Lucy:

You have been tested & have passed the test.

KINGDOM
Women

Encountering God and Living in His Presence

Powerful encounters are to come!

ONDINA LASZLO

Ondina Laszlo.

Our Mission

Called to bring the supernatural power of God to this generation.

Kingdom Women – Volume 3
Encountering God and Living in His Presence
(A Message Every Woman Needs to Know)

Edition: October 2017
ISBN: 978-1-59272-701-8

Unless otherwise indicated, all Scripture quotations are taken from the Holy Bible, New International Version®, NIV® Copyright © 1973, 1978, 1984, 2011 by Biblica, Inc.® Used by permission. All rights reserved worldwide. Scripture quotations marked (NKJV) are taken from the New King James Version, © 1979, 1980, 1982, 1984 by Thomas Nelson, Inc. Used by permission. Amplified Bible, Classic Edition (AMPC) Copyright © 1954, 1958, 1962, 1964, 1965, 1987 by The Lockman Foundation. Scripture quotations marked (AMP) are taken from the Amplified® Bible, © 1954, 1958, 1962, 1964, 1965, 1987 by The Lockman Foundation. Used by permission. (www.Lockman.org).

Project Director: Andres Brizuela

General Editor: José M. Anhuaman

Editor: Jessica Galarreta

Spanish Translation: Gloria Zura

Cover Design: Danielle Cruz Nieri

Interior Design: Caroline Pereira

Category: Supernatural / Spiritual Growth

King Jesus International Ministry
14100 SW 144th Avenue, Miami, FL 33186
Tel: (305) 382-3171 - Fax: (305) 675-5770
Printed in the United States of America

Index

Dedication

I dedicate this book to all the powerful men and women of God, spiritual leaders that have impacted my life by means of their love and fear of God, their exemplary lives, and by the revelation they carry. Each one has served as an influence and example to follow. Some of them I have known personally, others I have not known personally, nevertheless, I received an impartation of what God deposited in their lives through what they ministered.

I can include in this list many people, but I want to specifically mention Apostle Guillermo Maldonado and Prophet Ana Maldonado, who have been my spiritual parents for over 20 years; my natural father, Reverend Orlando Perdomo, who led me to Christ and was my Pastor for the first 25 years of my life, Pastor Kenneth Hagin, who has since gone to be with the Lord, Pastor Benny Hinn, Evangelist Billy Graham, Prophet Cathy Lechner, Apostle Alan Vincent, Apostle Bill Hamon, Prophet Cindy Jacobs, Apostle Renny McLean, Dr. Marina McLean, and Teacher Joyce Meyer, just to mention a few. May God repay each of you richly for your contribution in maturing the body of Christ, which included maturing me.

Acknowledgements

I am eternally grateful to the Holy Spirit; if it had not been for the Holy Spirit's intervention in my life, I would not be whole, free, secure, or feel fulfilled with the life God has given me. Without His Spirit's guidance, I would not have been able to develop a strong relationship with God the Father.

I also want to thank my husband, Jose Arturo Laszlo. Without his support, shown in many ways, I could not have written this series of books entitled "Kingdom Women". I thank you honey for being obedient to God, and allowing me to do what God asked of me.

Prologue

I am so thankful that God has laid these volumes of Kingdom Women in the heart of Teacher Ondina Laszlo. She has served in ministry with Apostle Maldonado and Prophet Ana, so she knows firsthand the importance of having a relationship with God first, so that we are able to persevere all the onslaught of the enemy.

Kingdom women all over the world, from different backgrounds and circumstances, all face the same trials. We have to balance home, spouse, children, finances, cooking, praying, serving in church etc... All these responsibilities can be time consuming, and they all have a place in our priorities. However, they cannot get accomplished with peace, joy and a sound mind without the presence of God being first in our thoughts.

Teacher Ondina addresses all the factors that we walk through as women, and she gives us no excuse to live beneath a worshipful awareness of the Lord our God.

We all encounter struggles, but our will to survive sometimes comes with endurance, and not enjoyment. I love this volume of

Kingdom Women, because it gives us clear strategies that I know we can apply to our daily walk and discipline with the Lord.

My friend, this is an awakening for you, to become the Kingdom woman that leads by example. Take the territory of your mind and have it renewed again to conquer and overcome the enemy's plan that wants to keep you defeated.

Thank you for bringing this resource to women of service in the Kingdom.

Dr. Marina McLean
Co- Founder of RMM, Dallas, Texas

Introduction

During one of my intimate prayer times with the Lord, I heard Him speak to me clearly, and He affirmed the purpose of this 3rd Volume of this series of books entitled, "Kingdom Women." I clearly heard Him tell me: "Take the women into intimacy, lead them into My presence." In addition, the Lord said, "Again I speak change and transformation, from one level of glory to another. You have led so many women already through a process of change from their mentalities of crisis, from the mentalities that restricted them in their hearts and in their minds. Now you must take them into intimacy with Me and lead them into My presence. Lead them to security, to a sense of son-ship. Lead them to renew their minds by establishing My word in them, so that they may be rooted and grounded in My Word and in My love, in My unfailing love, and in My faithfulness, which will never leave them abandoned. They will never be let down by Me or feel discouraged. If discouragement comes, it is not because of Me. I discourage no one; I uplift all who come to Me."

By the grace of God, this book will fulfill its purpose, which is that you allow the Holy Spirit to guide and direct you to be in

God's presence every day, enjoying a fulfilling, intimate relationship with Him. If you have lost your passion for God, it will be rekindled by God's supernatural grace.

Are you ready to go into a further place of intimacy with God?

Chapter 1

Encountering God and His Goodness

We were created by God to abide in His presence, however, we will know God only when we encounter Him. Every time we encounter God, we become more intimately acquainted with Him. You may ask, "what is an encounter with God?" An encounter with God is an experience within the atmosphere that God moves in and where the Father commences to reveal Himself and all His glory. The glory of God is more than just one attribute of God, it is the Lord God Himself in all His intrinsic and eternal perfection, the sum of His attributes and the totality of His majesty. God's glory is who He is, what He possesses, and what He is like. Therefore, an encounter with God is an experience with His presence, with His power, with His love, with His goodness, with God Himself. Our minds are unable to understand God, but we will encounter Him and become one with Him as we set all distractions aside for a time, in order to seek Him. We will progressively come into a deeper unity and intimacy with God, and we will grow closer to Him as we spend more time in His presence.

Up to now, your plans might not have included investing time to get to know God and establishing communion with Him, resulting in an inconsistent relationship with God throughout most of your life. In fact, you may have sought Him only when you faced difficulties in the past. If that has been your experience, you are not alone. Unfortunately, the emphasis, in many Christian circles, has not been placed in having a personal relationship with God or establishing intimacy with Him, or in experiencing all that He wants to give us through the finished work of Christ on the cross and His resurrection power. Instead, many Christians are focused on mundane things and consequently, they have settled for a superficial relationship with God, never getting to know Him personally, and only seeking Him in times of crisis. It is my prayer that as you read this book, the Holy Spirit will impress you to make the decision to seek God so as to ignite a passion for Him, the Lord of Glory, the God that loves you; and to have a heart that seeks His presence with a deep desire to please Him. Not only is this my prayer, it is also God's will for you and the best thing that can happen in your life. Achieving this unity with Him will supply you with everything you need. The results you will gain will far outweigh any personal sacrifice or time investment that you make.

The knowledge of God vs. the knowledge of evil

Evil is all around us and our failure to seek God, who is the source of all that is good, as stated in James 1:17, automatically results in evil affecting every area of our lives. In order to remain untouched by the evil that is prevalent all around us, we need to decide every day to draw close to God and know Him, since the knowledge or experience of God is the knowledge or experience of good. Evil was released upon the earth through man's disobedience to God, and its consequence is death. God, instead, is the source of life. Jesus said, *"I am the way and the truth and the life"* (John 14:6). (See also Jeremiah 9:23-24 and Romans 12:2). From the beginning, it was not God's intention that we know or experience evil. In the book of Genesis, we read that He told Adam and Eve not to eat of the tree of knowledge of good and evil. *"But **you must not eat** from the tree of the **knowledge** of good and evil, for when you eat from it you will **certainly die**"* (Genesis 2:17).

God was not threatening Adam and Eve when He told them they would surely die if they ate of the tree of the knowledge of good and evil, He was merely stating a fact, He was stating an eternal truth; that if they ate of it, the knowledge of evil would bring them death. In spite of it, they chose to experience evil in the same way we continue to choose to experience evil today; by choosing to be separated from God. Nevertheless, God still gives us a choice to depart from evil, rebuke it and cast it out. Proverbs says: *"Be not wise in your own eyes; reverently fear and worship the Lord and turn [entirely] away from evil"* (Proverbs 3:7 AMPC). Please note that in this verse we are told we can choose to depart from evil, which means we can also choose to experience evil.

15

What is evil?

Evil is all wickedness, what is hurtful, what is wrong, what causes trouble, affliction, illness, adversity, something harmful, grievous and sad, disagreeable, malignant, bad, unpleasant, that which causes pain, unhappiness, misery, that which is displeasing, unkind, that causes distress, injury, and calamity.

No one in their right mind would voluntarily choose to experience all of these calamities. However, every time we choose to be independent of God we are, in reality, choosing to experience evil. God's plan to deliver us from evil was and is for His kingdom to be established in every area of our lives (see Matthew 6:9-15). When the kingdom of God is established in a person, a place or a city, it brings righteousness, peace, and joy (see Romans 14:17).

> *Pray, then, in this way: 'Our Father who is in heaven, hallowed be Your name. 'Your kingdom come. Your will be done, on earth as it is in heaven. 'Give us this day our daily bread. 'And forgive us our debts, as we also have forgiven our debtors. (Letting go of both the wrong and the resentment.) 'And do not lead us into temptation, but **deliver us from evil**. [For yours is the kingdom and the power and the glory forever. Amen.'] – Matthew 6:9-13 NASB*

The devil's intention from the beginning was to prohibit mankind from receiving God's goodness, from having a relationship with Him and living in His presence, under submission to His kingdom. From the onset, the devil designed a plan to prevent man from enjoying God's tender mercies, loving-kindness and from moving in His glorious power. The way Satan accomplished this separation between God and man in the Garden of Eden was by using carefully crafted words and making statements that cast a negative light on God's character, to introduce doubt in the minds of Adam and Eve about God's true nature. Satan caused Eve to negatively view God's command by making her believe that God was not being fair with her and Adam. The serpent may have sarcastically told her: "How just like God to withhold the fruit of the best tree from you." He guided Eve to doubt God's goodness. He introduced false ideas in her mind, which caused doubt, mistrust, and disbelief.

Even today, in the same way as in the Garden of Eden, the devil's words are still carefully crafted to cast doubt about God's character in our minds. Many people have no desire to seek God today because their perception of Him has been ruined as a result of the lies that have misrepresented His true character, and they have no expectations of receiving anything good from Him.

Satan diligently works to dishonor God in the eyes of His people with false accusations and elaborate fabricated lies, intended to discourage them from seeking God and to defraud them of a close relationship with Him, in order to steal, cheat and deprive God's people of the true love, power, peace, joy, blessings and all the goodness God sent Jesus to freely give us. Today, more than ever, it is important to discern the lies presented to our minds and recognize them for what they are: deceptive ideas about God's true character. We need to be on our guard in order to not fall for Satan's deceit regarding the nature and character of our God, especially during these end times that we now live in, where deceit is rampant. 1 Timothy 4:1 states, *"The Spirit clearly says that in later times some will abandon the faith and follow deceiving spirits and things taught by demons."*

Has the devil discredited God in your eyes?

It is imperative we think rightly about God and know Him as He truly is, in order to relate to Him. Until now, has your perception of God been erroneous? Have you kept your heart far from Him because you perceive Him as being harsh or unfair? To determine if this has happened to you, ask yourself the following questions: Am I expecting God to do good things in my life based on my genuine faith in His character? Have the problems I have gone through in the course of life, influenced me to think negatively about God and my future? Have I lost hope in receiving God's blessings and prosperity?

When you are expecting something bad to happen, you can be certain that expectation is being provoked by the devil, and it can open the door for Satan to bring to your life the bad things you are anticipating. However, when you expect by faith to receive good things from God, you open the door to God's plans for your life. God wants to show you His nature, He wants to express Himself to you, how He is, and His glory. He wants to show you His goodness and loving kindness. He desires that you experience today who He truly is.

> *And therefore the Lord [earnestly] waits [expecting, looking, and longing] to be gracious to you; and therefore He*

lifts Himself up, that He may have mercy on you and show loving-kindness to you. For the Lord is a God of justice. Blessed (happy, fortunate, to be envied) are all those who [earnestly] wait for Him, who expect and look and long for Him [for His victory, His favor, His love, His peace, His joy, and His matchless, unbroken companionship]!
– Isaiah 30:18 AMPC

What do you think God is like?

God has a prevalent state of mind and way of being. He lives in a certain type of atmosphere and has a consistent attitude. His mood is consistently good and cheerful, pleasant and amiable. He is friendly, kind, gracious and full of love! He possesses a sweetness that is unique to Him. He has a pleasant disposition and is kindhearted, God is good. His composure is always benevolent. God does not have a sullen, ill-tempered mental state; nor is He in a bad mood. God is not mad at you! He is balanced in nature. He is perfect.

God is good-humored. This is His continuous tendency and inclination. God is not given to unpredictable changes of mood, especially not sudden spurts of anger, or irritability, instead, He is patient with us so that we may repent. (See 2 Peter 3:9). He is not temperamental nor is He moody. God is not volatile nor capricious. God's mood is not unpredictable. He is good all the time! *"For the Lord is good; His mercy and loving-kindness are everlasting, His faithfulness and truth endure to all generations."* (Psalm 100:5 AMPC)

God is not quick to punish or find fault. He is not quick to condemn. He is not quick to criticize, rebuke and reprimand. Instead, He is quick to encourage, believe in us and forgive us. His correction is never mixed with rejection or disdain. He corrects us with love. (See Hebrews 12:6).

God is not disapproving. He believes in us and endorses us. He acknowledges our efforts to please Him when we approach Him in faith. He is gracious, and He is not hard to please. (See Hebrews 11:6).

> *But from everlasting to everlasting the Lord's love is with those who fear him, and his righteousness with their children's children. – Psalm 103:17*

God's will is to bring the glory of His Kingdom to earth by establishing the two main aspects that govern it, which are: first, the Kingdom of God is founded on His benevolent rule and His love as our heavenly Father, and second: The Kingdom of God is supernatural and operates under the power and the glory of its King.

God is looking and longing for someone who is waiting for Him to be good to them. God wants to be good to you, He wants you to know Him and experience His glory, all that He is. However, you must develop faith in God's goodness and be expecting Him to move in your life.

God is good. Everything He does is good and wonderful. Our expectations should be based on His benevolence and not the circumstances that surround us. God wants to do something wonderful in your life every day. However, you need to put your faith in His unfailing character and be expectant for it to happen.

> *How abundant are the good things that you have stored up*
> *for those who fear you that you bestow in the sight of all,*
> *on those who take refuge in you. – Psalm 31:19*

Hindrances to believing in God's goodness

Has a bad circumstance in your life made you believe that God is unkind and uncaring? Having experienced many disappointments throughout your life may have focused you on the circumstances and impossibilities that surround you, and all the hurtful events you have gone through, and you may unconsciously blame God for having allowed these things to happen to you. Have you been projecting onto God, and ascribing to Him, the negative qualities and the experiences you have had with toxic people who have hurt you; who are hard to please, self-seeking, unfair, unjust, demanding and unapproving? These experiences may have already made you a negative person who is continuously anticipating more bad things to come your way. You may have already been subconsciously blaming God for the bad you have undergone, which He has not caused and is so unlike His character.

In many inner healing and deliverance sessions where I have ministered, the Holy Spirit has led me to have the people that are present confess forgiveness towards God, not because God is guilty of having done something wrong to them, but because some of the people present have been carrying a grudge against Him. In their eyes, He was not there for them when they expected Him to be, or He did not defend them the way they thought He should have defended them.

Do not blame God any longer for the things you have gone through! He is a loving God. He was not the author of the bad you went through. It is clear in God's word that we are not to live in gloom because God is kind, good and full of mercy! He has always been this way and He will always be the same.

- All that God is and does is good. *You are good, and what you do is good; teach me your decrees.* (Psalm 119:68)
- God's goodness and love last forever. *Give thanks to the Lord, for he is good; his love endures forever.* (Psalm 107:1)
- God is good to everyone. *The Lord is good to all; he has compassion on all he has made.* (Psalm 145:9)
- All things that are good are from God. *Every good and perfect gift is from above, coming down from the Father of the heavenly lights, who does not change like shifting shadows.* (James 1:17)
- God does not withhold his blessings from you. *For the LORD God is a sun and shield; the Lord bestows favor and honor; no good thing does he withhold from those whose walk is blameless.* (Psalm 84:11)
- We are blessed through God's goodness. *Taste and see that the Lord is good; blessed is the one who takes refuge in him.* (Psalm 34:8)
- His goodness leads us to live holy lives. *Or do you despise*

the riches of His goodness, forbearance, and longsuffering, not knowing that the goodness of God leads you to repentance? (Romans 2:4 NKJV)

By these and many other scriptures, we can be certain that what God does is good for us, what He does is pleasing, what He does is beneficial, what He does causes joy, and He is our loving heavenly Father!

God's goodness is not pending to be proven

It is an irrevocable truth that has already been established. Have you been waiting and expecting certain things from God and holding unto them as if they were the qualifiers to prove God's goodness? God has already qualified as being good. God has already been gracious. Look and see what God has already done. Give Him thanks for what He has already done. We cannot withhold thanksgiving and praise to God waiting for certain circumstances to change. We need to praise and worship God for what He has already done by His great mercy and grace.

It takes faith in God's goodness to anticipate good in our lives; likewise, we must have faith that God is working all things out for our own good, no matter what the current circumstances look like.

And we know that in all things God works for the good of those who love him, who have been called according to his purpose. – Romans 8:28

It is time to receive the truth and expose Satan's cunning work for what it is: a lie. Do not allow yourself to be beguiled any longer. You have been fed untrue accusations about God so that you would perceive Him differently from how He truly is. Today you can renounce these lies, which are toxins that cause spiritual hardness in your heart and hinder your relationship with God.

I invite you to declare the following prayer out loud:

Father God, I renounce every lie from the devil that I have believed, every wrong concept that I have had of Your character and nature so that Your Holy Spirit can enlighten me with the revelation of how You truly are. Father, I forgive You and release You from all blame that I have subconsciously accused you of. I recognize today that You were not the author of the painful experiences I have gone through in my life. I believe that today, You will set me free from all lies I have believed regarding Your character and I humble myself to be renewed in my mind by Your Word and Your Holy Spirit who lead me to all truth.

Since You, oh God, are eternal, the God of the past, present and future, I anticipate goodness, grace and favor to follow me all the days of my life, today and in the future. I will not have a pessimistic attitude in my heart. I will not have lack, I will have abundance. I will not be ashamed, I will be placed on high.

You are a Faithful and Good God. Your mercies are new

every morning. I receive Your good works today and for my future. I anticipate good and I do not stop considering You a good God when You do not answer my prayers immediately. In fact, I have complete confidence and faith in whom I have believed; You are faithful to complete everything that You have started. I voluntarily change my perspective of You and align it to Your word. May I see Your goodness and Your grace continuously, may I look upon it, may my heart turn to it so that I can remain grateful, that my mind and heart be convinced of Your faithfulness, and that there be no room for doubt.

Father God, I declare that every doubt about Your character is removed from my mind, my conscious and subconscious right now in the name of Jesus. I renounce to doubt and I believe in Your goodness. You are a good God. My future and my present belong to You. I yield my present and my future to You. I trust You with my life and my family. I trust You to direct my life and govern over it. I know that in Your kingdom there is abundance of good and there is no evil. I live in Your kingdom where you rule over me.

Father God, eradicate all evil and all doubt, take it out of my life, take it out of my soul, take it out of my will and emotions, my conscious mind and my subconscious mind. Destroy the works of Satan, destroy what he has built up for years, all his conniving lies, and bring Your kingdom, Your rule, government peace and joy, and everything Your kingdom represents in a greater way into my life.

May I not focus on the circumstances that surround me, may I not be mindful of the people that have hurt me. May I not see those that are burdensome and harsh. May I see past them and their humanity, past those who oppose Your will. I see past those who speak against me. I see Your goodness, I see Your grace, I see Your favor and I receive it as a little child. I receive from Your mercy. I receive from You Your love and grace and every good gift, every perfect gift from above. I receive it now and appropriate myself of it. I do not have to wait to see if God will be good to me, You are good to me today. I receive my inheritance of Your good will, Your good intentions and Your good thoughts towards me. I receive Your good plans, your perfect plans, I receive every good gift from above that Jesus died to give me.

I thank You for abundantly caring for me. I thank You for abundantly providing for me, I thank You for abundantly having mercy upon me. I thank You for Your grace over me, Your infinite grace that saved me, Your infinite grace that sustains me, Your infinite grace that has upheld me and has protected me. I thank You, my God, that You have not left me an orphan, I thank You for Your Holy Spirit. I thank You for the blood of Jesus that I can activate. I activate it now in my home and over every possession, in my family, the blood of Jesus cleanses and undoes sin. I thank You for the inheritance of the name of Jesus. Thank You for the power and the authority of that name. I receive all of these good gifts, these gracious gifts, which Jesus died to give me. I thank You for You have given me abundance.

Say out loud!

*I will **not** anticipate evil – I will always anticipate good because my God is good! Amen.*

Give thanks to the Lord, for he is good. His love endures forever. – Psalm 136:1

God is determined to bless you!

A blessing is not wishful thinking or nice words. It is a holy convocation that calls the power of God to come upon us. When God blesses you, His favor, His grace, His protection and His provision meet you where you are.

Praise be to the God and Father of our Lord Jesus Christ, *who has blessed us **in the heavenly realms with every spiritual blessing **in Christ**. – Ephesians 1:3***

The word blessing in the Greek word "eulogy" means: God has pronounced good things for our benefit. He has decreed them. An official order and an official proclamation have gone out from God to bless us.

Some spiritual blessings are:

- **Holiness:** God has chosen to make us holy and blameless because of His love, His good pleasure, and His grace.
- **Adoption:** We have full status as His children, with all the benefits thereof. (See John 1:12)
- **Grace and Favor:** We have received grace and favor

through Christ, the beloved of God.

- **Redeemed:** We have been redeemed. Redemption speaks of buying one's freedom, this means we are no longer obligated to be slaves to sin.
- **Spiritual Inheritance:** The inheritance that is given to us through Christ. *"What no eye has seen, what no ear has heard, and what no human mind has conceived' –the things God has prepared for those who love him"* (1 Corinthians 2:9). This spiritual inheritance includes the riches of His glory, the presence of God, and an eternal home.
- **The Holy Spirit:** The seal of the Holy Spirit, God's mark of ownership.

We have been blessed with all spiritual blessings in Christ Jesus!

> *You will be blessed when you come in and blessed when you go out. The Lord will grant that the enemies who rise up against you will be defeated before you. They will come at you from one direction but flee from you in seven. The Lord will send a blessing on your barns and on everything you put your hand to. The Lord your God will bless you in the land he is giving you. – Deuteronomy 28:6-8*

You can walk blessed and highly favored

The goodness and mercy of God will follow you wherever you are as you dwell in His presence every day. *"Surely your goodness and love will follow me all the days of my life, and I will dwell in the house of the Lord forever"* (Psalm 23:6). **The goodness and mercy of God are not just following after you passively,**

it pursues after you passionately. God is determined to bless you, therefore His goodness and mercy chase after you. In other words, not only will goodness and mercy follow you all the days of your life but as you continuously dwell in the presence of the Lord (as you make His presence your dwelling place), the goodness and mercy that follows you will increase, it will become greater in quality, quantity, and intensity. We need to acknowledge the goodness and mercy of God we receive every day with thanksgiving. As you remain in the presence of the Lord every day, you will notice an increase in the type of goodness and mercy received from one day to another. *"The path of the righteous is like the morning sun, shining ever brighter till the full light of day"* (Proverbs 4:18) You will start to receive the best. You will begin to receive what is good in the widest sense of the word.

God is not only good, He is generous and extravagant

God loves to lavish His gifts on His children. He gives the desires of their hearts to them that love Him. (See Psalm 37:4). God is good in the widest sense of the word. He gives the best, what is beautiful, what is better, what is fine, the most pleasant and the most precious. He gives prosperity, wealth, and welfare. God is overgenerous with His mercy and favor on those that seek Him, beyond what is usual.

Dear reader, do not withstand or resist God's goodness any longer with unbelief and lack of expectancy. As you dwell in God's presence in your daily prayer time, you need to expect greater gifts from Him and not resist them through unbelief.

If you apply your reasoning to all the impossibilities that exist, you will be unable to receive God's best.

Our expectancy needs to be on God's unfailing character, not on our merit of it. Everything we have is because of His grace that has made us righteous through the sacrifice of Jesus. To receive God's favor, we must believe that He desires to reward those who seek Him. Without faith, we are not able to receive His grace, or the good things He wants to give us, and it is impossible to please Him to receive his favor: *"But without faith it is impossible to please Him, for he who comes to God must believe that He is (He is good, He is love, He is faithful etc.) and that He is a rewarder of those who diligently seek Him"* (Hebrews 11:6). In other words, He rewards those who employ themselves to diligently seek Him; those who attempt to find Him, desire to obtain Him and ask for His presence to come.

God is almighty, He exceeds everything

In addition to His goodness, God is almighty and able to do what far surpasses our limited knowledge, our finite understanding, and even exceed that which is recorded in scripture. John concludes his gospel saying that the whole world would not have enough room for the books that would be written if all the works of Christ were recorded.

Abraham was aware of God's goodness and faithfulness and of His great power. As he experienced God and developed a relationship with Him, he became certain of two things: First, he considered God to be faithful (see Hebrews 11:11), and secondly, he reasoned that God was almighty because he thought to himself that God could raise Isaac from the dead if needed. (See Hebrews 11:17). In a similar way, as we experience God and develop a close relationship with Him, we will come to know Him as faithful and infinitely powerful.

God is able to exceeds your expectations!

He is able to do exceedingly above all you can ask or imagine. (Ephesians 3:20) states, *"Now to him who is **able** to do immeasurably more than all we ask or imagine, according to his power that is at work within us."* The word "able" in this verse describes that which has sufficient or necessary power, means, skill, or resources to accomplish His objective. Therefore "able" means that God is powerful enough and has the ability to perform what He has promised. God's ability is expressed by His omnipotence and His glory. God can take any bad circumstance and turn it around!

Throughout the Scriptures, God's great power, His glory, majesty, strength, mighty acts, glorious splendor, and wondrous works are consistently referenced together with His benevolent goodness. When God's glorious and powerful works are spoken about in the Scriptures, you will find that consistently His goodness and His desire to extend His kindness and tender mercies towards man are also emphasized.

Declare his glory among the nations, his marvelous deeds among all peoples. For great is the Lord and most worthy of praise... Splendor and majesty are before him; strength

*and joy are in his dwelling place. [...] Give thanks to the Lord, **for he is good**; his love endures forever.*
– 1 Chronicles 16:24-25, 27, 34

God's power and glory are connected with His benevolence

*Give thanks to the Lord, **for he is good**. His love endures forever. [...] to Him who alone does great wonders, His love endures forever. Who by his understanding made the heavens, His love endures forever. Who spread out the earth upon the waters, His love endures forever. – Psalm 136:1, 4-6*

*One generation commends your works to another; they tell of your mighty acts. They speak of the glorious splendor of your majesty— and I will meditate on your wonderful works. They tell of the power of your awesome works— and I will proclaim your great deeds. They celebrate **Your abundant goodness** and joyfully sing of your righteousness. The Lord is gracious and compassionate, slow to anger and rich in love. **The Lord is good to all**; he has compassion on all he has made. – Psalm 145:4-9*

The answer to your prayers and the breakthrough you have been waiting for will be the result of what God has been doing all this time behind the scenes, that you have not seen. Whether you see it or not, whether you feel it or not, keep expecting God's goodness and His intervention, keep giving thanks to Him because He is longing to be good to you and His power is unlimited. He wants you to believe something good is going to happen to you today.

When we diligently seek God, our lives and the atmosphere where we live will be charged with His love and His blessings. Wherever there is a Kingdom woman that establishes the Kingdom of God first in her own life, and then in her home, evil will not prevail. Apostle Maldonado states in his book, "The Kingdom of God and its Righteousness" that both, the Kingdom of God (His goodness) and the kingdom of darkness (evil) are established on earth by mankind; he also states, "man is the only being who can decide which kingdom will govern his life… Are you willing to become that man or woman who chooses to establish the Kingdom of God on Earth?"

Chapter 2

The Battle for
your Heart

Eternal life is not knowledge of God, it is to know God personally.

> Now this is eternal life: that **they know** you, the only true
> God, and Jesus Christ, whom you have sent. – John 17:3

Please note that John 17:3 states that eternal life does not consist in merely acknowledging that God exists, instead it states that we should know Him personally.

Jesus was asked: *"Teacher... what must I do to inherit eternal life?"* (Luke 10:25). Let's look at Jesus' answer in Luke 10:26-28: "What is written in the Law?" he replied. "How do you read it?" He answered, "'Love the Lord your God with all your heart and with all your soul and with all your strength and with all your mind'; and, 'Love your neighbor as yourself.'" "You have answered correctly," Jesus replied. "Do this and you will live." (You will have eternal life).

The desire of God the Father for all humanity is that we might know the love of God by experience, through Christ, and be filled with Him, and thereby be full of His power. He desires that Christ may dwell in the hearts of each and every person, through faith; that *"being rooted and established in love, may have power, together with all the Lord's holy people, to grasp how wide and long and high and deep is the love of Christ, and to know this love that surpasses knowledge—that you may be filled to the measure of all the fullness of God."* (Ephesians 3:17-19).

In the book of Ephesians, Apostle Paul emphasizes the importance of having a personal experience with the Godhead. Please note that he does not promote knowledge of doctrine as the means to relate with God, instead he stresses the value of receiving revelation of the Father of glory –which includes receiving the spirit of wisdom–, and states that we are to know things such as the riches of the glory of God's inheritance in the saints, and the exceeding greatness of His power toward those who believe. He speaks of the importance of our experiencing the working of His mighty power, which He worked in Christ when He raised Him from the dead and seated Him at His right hand in heavenly places, far above all principality, power, might, dominion, and every name that is named, not only in this age but also in that which is to come. (See Ephesians 1:17-23).

Experiencing God's eternal life

Eternal life is not just life that does not die and continues forever, it is the very nature of God, which penetrates our humanity and unites us with Him. In 1 John chapter 1, Apostle John begins to speak of a special kind of life of which he had heard, seen with his own eyes and felt with his hands, which was from the beginning. He had seen this special kind of life in the Word of life, Jesus Christ Himself.

> *That which was from the beginning, which we have heard, which we have seen with our eyes, which we have looked upon, and our hands have handled, concerning the Word of life— **the life was manifested, and we have seen, and bear witness**, and declare to you that eternal life which was with the Father and was manifested to us— that which we have seen and heard we declare to you, that you also may have fellowship with us; and truly **our fellowship is with the Father and with His Son Jesus Christ**. –1 John 1:1-3 NKJV*

When you received Jesus as your Lord and Savior and confessed that He rose from the dead (Romans 10:9), you received eternal life. Now you can put into action that eternal life that Christ Jesus has given you, and it will manifest as it did when the Apostles of the New Testament activated it.

> *Whoever has the Son has life; whoever does not have the Son of God does not have life. –1 John 5:12*

Through this eternal life we have, we can see God's great

power, as did the disciples of Jesus. The Apostle John says that he heard, saw with his eyes, looked and felt this life with his hands because he walked with Jesus. How can we do all these things: hear, see, contemplate, and feel with our hands, God's eternal life and put it into practice?

Keys to experience the eternal life

The Apostle John in 1 John 2:12-14, gives us keys to enjoy and experience the eternal life that has already been given to us by God. There are three things that we must continually be. The correct word is "to be" not "to do". He states that we are to be:

1. **Small children:** Children are innocent. God reveals all things to those who are pure in heart, as are children. Small children are pure in heart because their sins have been forgiven and they are righteous. Also, because they have been given an identity by their heavenly Father. They know God as their Father.

2. **Fathers:** Fathers are the children of God who have reached maturity. Those who are mature in Christ have a profound knowledge of the Word of God (Jesus Christ) which is from the beginning. He is the one who gives this eternal life. 1 John 2:14 says: *"I write to you, fathers, because you know him who is from the beginning."*

In the beginning was the Word, and the Word was with God, and the Word was God [...] Through him all things were made... In him was life, and that life was the light of all mankind. John 1:1, 3-4)

3. **Young men or young warriors:** *"...because you have over-come the evil one"* (1 John 2:13). To experience this eternal life to its fullest, we must be willing to become warriors ready to fight against Satan in the name of Jesus.

In other words, according to Apostle John, if you have a pure heart, if you know God as your Father, if you know that you are righteous, you know Jesus Christ as He is (victorious and all powerful), if you have reached a level of spiritual maturity and you know what God has given you —eternal life—, if you know God's Word, if you are ready to fight and overcome the evil one and if you have an identity given to you by your heavenly Father, then you can and will have daily experiences with the abundant benefits of God's eternal life, which you have not yet tapped into. All those benefits were in Christ, were experienced by the disciples of Jesus, and God has given them to you also.

The good thing about this eternal life that God has given us, is that it is not limited by the laws of time and matter. It is born of God, comes from God, and as such, overcomes the world.

> *For everyone born of God overcomes the world. This is the victory that has overcome the world, even our faith. [...] And this is the testimony: **God has given us eternal life**, and this life is in His Son. Whoever has the Son has life...*
> *– 1 John 5:4, 11-12*

> *I write these things to you who believe in the name of the Son of God so that you may know that you have eternal life. This is the confidence we have in approaching God:*

*that if we ask anything according to his will, he hears us.
And if we know that he hears us—whatever we ask—we
know that we have what we asked of him. – 1 John 5:13-15*

Experiences with the manifestation of God's eternal life

I would like to quickly share some of the most recent experiences I have had with the manifestation of God's eternal life as I believed God to manifest His love and His power:

- God led me to declare over a couple that owned a building they had been trying to sell for five years but were unable to, that they would have multiple offers in a few weeks. They came to tell me two weeks later that they received three offers from people who wanted to buy their building!
- While I ministered the Word at a class, God led me to release supernatural finances. I told the students in attendance that whoever received that declaration by faith, would receive supernatural unexpected finances. A woman that had been in that class came to me to testify that the day after that class, she received an unexpected large sum of money supernaturally.
- I received a word of knowledge while ministering, that a person was addicted to nicotine and that God was going to remove that addiction, and also remove the taste of nicotine from their mouth. A man came forward to testify that I spoke of him, and that he was set free.
- At another time, I personally experienced how God healed the eyesight of six different people instantly. I tested all of them and confirmed that they could now see what they

could not see before they were prayed for.

- I prayed for a man who was deaf in one ear; as soon as I declared healing over his ear and then tested his hearing, he was so surprised as he testified that he could now hear what he was not able to hear before from the ear that had been deaf!

- On another occasion, two women came suffering with intense pain. One of them had been enduring pain from arthritis in one knee for over a year, and the other had been getting pain in her back and neck for months. God instantly healed them both. Those things they could not do before without suffering great pain, they were now able to do painlessly.

- At another time, I prayed for a woman who could not kneel for months because of the pain in both her knees. She was healed immediately and to show she had received her miracle, she knelt down with tears of joy in her eyes.

- There was a man who said he had been suffering with abdominal pain for a long time. He said the doctors could not tell him the reason for the pain. I prayed for him, and the pain left him immediately.

- Even over the telephone, God's eternal life manifests. While praying a deliverance prayer for a couple over the telephone, they testified that they were set free from the oppression that was upon them.

- I prayed for a woman who is a House of Peace (HOP) leader at our church. She had come to tell me that each time she had HOP at her house, she would experience oppression (fear, anxiety, sadness, etc.) afterwards in her house and in her personal life, which she never experienced before.

She said she felt this oppression came because the people that would come to receive at her House of Peace were oppressed with all these things. I prayed a prayer of authority over her to take dominion over every spiritual oppression in people coming into her home. She called me that same week to testify that there was a complete transformation at her house, and a change in her HOP, and that there was no more oppression and she felt the difference.

- I prayed for a man who had osteoarthritis (a degenerative joint disease) for the past four years and who could hardly walk. Because of it, he could not go up and down stairs. After I prayed for him, he went up and down stairs four times without any pain.

These are just a few testimonies of God's eternal life in action. As we renew our minds to the truth that we possess God's eternal life in us, we can manifest it wherever we go. However, when we do not renew our way of thinking about the eternal life that we already have, we are unable to experience the power of the life of God that is in us. We are unable to see that through this eternal life, whatever we ask of God the Father according to His will, we will have it.

The renewal of the mind

The renewal of the mind concerning God's eternal life that is in us, and the power of faith unleashed through this renewal of our mind, are only possible for consecrated and persistent believers who sincerely desire to live a powerful and holy life. The renewal of the mind is not realized by Christians who obey

God only when it suits them. The renewing of the mind is only achieved by the believer who really gives his life completely to Jesus Christ. It is only for the believer who loves the truth and wants to be transformed according to the Word of God, and also see a change in their circumstances. The renewal of the mind is not for those who have no interest in knowing God on a deeper level.

Pastor David Yonggi Cho stated in his book *The Fourth Dimension* - Volume Two: *"The minds of Christians ... can be renewed so that our potential can be realized as human beings created in the image of God. We will then be able to... transcend limitations, our capacity is limited only by our own limits."*

Why are so many christians unable to transcend limitations?

The answer to this question is that your mind is continually influenced by the world. The world and your old man lead you to doubt God, to fear, to be insecure, to see limitations, to reason, to see things as impossible, instead of totally believing in God and His power.

Apostle Guillermo Maldonado stated in his book entitled: *How to Walk in the Supernatural Power of God* the following: "It is essential to renew your mind so that you can have God's perspective and better bring the reality of heaven to earth. A mind that has not been renewed is unable to manifest the reality of that power on earth. When you renew your mind, you will be able to bring the reality of the supernatural world to earth and experience the will of God."

We can transcend the limitations of our mind and influence those around us as Jesus did, through God's eternal life that is in us. When Jesus walked on earth, He walked under open heavens and controlled the atmosphere around Him.

In his book entitled *Breaking the Intimidation,* John Bevere says: "Jesus could eat with sinners because He controlled the atmosphere. If you are stronger in God than the unbeliever is in the devil, you will control the atmosphere. If the sinner is more dominant in evil than the believer is in righteousness, the unbeliever will control the spiritual climate."

All of God's children can exercise this type of authority and walk as Jesus walked. Until you decide to renew your mind and implement the eternal life which you have in Christ, you will see little change or improvement in the circumstances around you, even though God's plan is to restore all things to you.

To walk in the power of this eternal life in Christ, you need to be in continuous contact with the author of life, God, our heavenly Father, through prayer. He will speak to your spirit and your heart and you will receive His way of thinking. He will guide you to live the life that Jesus lived here on earth; a life submissive and obedient, but also abundant and powerful.

Experience the power of eternal life through your words

God has given you His grace so that your words have creative power and can change circumstances. By God's grace through faith, you can cause a transformation to occur in your circumstances. Apostle Maldonado states in his book *How to Walk in the Supernatural Power of God* that when we have God's faith, "His Word in our mouths is the same as it is in His mouth".

Merely thinking words does not produce a miracle; the miracle is produced by saying what you believe. Christ promised us that we could only have what we confess. If we christians knew the power we unleash when we speak in faith, we could use our words more effectively. Just thinking thoughts of faith is not going to unleash the power of God, we must learn to speak with words of faith. Speak by faith what you have received through the Holy Spirit, with a clear goal for the future. When we receive instructions from the Holy Spirit, we can speak with authority to our chaotic situations and circumstances, and see how things will begin to happen.

Pastor David Yonggi Cho says in his book *The Fourth Dimension - Volume Two*: "In our society, we are faced with chaos all around us, just as the earth was chaotic (without form and void) before God spoke. As we learn to walk in obedience to the Holy Spirit, we will learn to use the creative ability of our words to bring order out of chaos"

The power to mobilize demons or angels

We need to set the wheels of creation into motion. Our tongue has the power to mobilize demons or angels. Which of the two are you mobilizing?

- **The power of your words:** *"The tongue has the power of life and death, and those who love it will eat its fruit."* (Proverbs 18:21)
- **The tongue can be used for evil:** *"Likewise, the tongue is a small part of the body, but it makes great boasts. Consider what a great forest is set on fire by a small spark. The tongue also is a fire, a world of evil among the parts of the body. It corrupts the whole body, sets the whole course of one's life on fire, and is itself set on fire by hell."* (James 3:5-6)
- **The tongue can be used for good:** *"My tongue will proclaim your righteousness, your praises all day long."* (Psalm 35:28)

Do you want your tongue to be used by the Holy Spirit to impact the circumstances around you? Through prayer and intercession, we can impact the world around us.

What makes our confession effective?

For your confession to be truly effective, you must have:

Faith in the power and authority of the name of Jesus:

His name has power in the heavens, on the earth and under the earth by the overwhelming victory that He obtained by means of His resurrection from the dead.

> *And being found in appearance as a man, he humbled himself by becoming obedient to death— even death on a cross! Therefore God exalted him to the highest place and gave him the name that is above every name, that at the name of Jesus every knee should bow, in heaven and on earth and under the earth. – Philippians 2:8-10*

According to this verse, there was a mystery in the death and resurrection of Jesus that the devil did not know. When Jesus died, and rose again, He received greater authority than He had when He walked on earth. He received authority in the heavens, on the earth and under the earth, where the powers of evil were established. The principalities and powers of evil established in the second heaven can only be overthrown by the power of the resurrection of Jesus Christ.

During the three days that Jesus was in hell after His death, the devil thought that the damage Jesus had done to Him was over. He said to himself: In the second heaven, I have principalities and powers and I can control the way people think on earth and now I have Jesus in hell, I'm secure. Jesus could not do me any real harm when He was on earth because only 120 people believed in Him after He was crucified so nothing has changed, I am still in power over mankind. But suddenly, a light penetrated hell, the glory of God, and the Spirit of God said: "Jesus you have no sin, arise and rise again!"

After His resurrection, all power was given to Jesus. Now it is not as when He walked on the earth. Before He had power only on earth, now He has power on earth, the heavens, and under the earth.

> *Then Jesus came to them and said, "All authority in heaven and on earth has been given to me. Therefore go and make disciples of all nations, baptizing them in the name of the Father and of the Son and of the Holy Spirit, and teaching them to obey everything I have commanded you.*

And surely I am with you always, to the very end of the age." – Matthew 28:18-20

That power Jesus received was not only to cast out demons on the earth, now he had power to undo the principalities and powers of evil in the heavenly places.

When Jesus resurrected, He took the keys of hell and death from the hands of Satan. The Scripture says, *"I am [Jesus] the Living One; I was dead, and now look, I am alive for ever and ever! And I hold the keys of death and Hades" (Revelation 1:18). Now, He stepped on his head, as it was written, "he will crush your head..."* (Genesis 3:15).

> *Who has gone into heaven and is at God's right hand—with angels, authorities and powers in submission to him.*
> *– 1 Peter 3:22*

> *And in Christ you have been brought to fullness. He is the head over every power and authority. – Colossians 2:10*

However, it does not end there. Now Jesus turns and gives the power of His name to His disciples and tells them:

> *And these signs will accompany those who believe: **In my name** they will drive out demons; they will speak in new tongues; they will pick up snakes with their hands; and when they drink deadly poison, it will not hurt them at all; they will place their hands on sick people, and they will get well. – Mark 16:17-18*

Very truly I tell you, whoever believes in me will do the works I have been doing, and they will do even greater things than these, because I am going to the Father. And I will do whatever you ask in my name, so that the Father may be glorified in the Son. You may ask me for anything in my name, and I will do it. – John 14:12-14

Many people are like Jesus' disciples when He was crucified. They are confused by the negativity they are experiencing, but also like the disciples after His resurrection, they will have a joy that no one can take away, and will conquer with the power of resurrection. Have an experience today with the risen and living Christ, exercise the eternal life that is in you through the decrees of your mouth; decrees of faith full of power, so that the will of God may be done on earth.

Passion for what you are praying:
The second thing you need to have for your confession to be truly effective, is that you must have passion for what you are praying: *"The tongue has the power of life and death, and those who love it will eat its fruit."* (Proverbs 18:21). You cannot establish that for which you have no passion for. That is why, the Scriptures say that God will give us the desires of our heart (Psalm 145:18-19) and also says in Mark 11:24, *"Therefore I tell you, whatever you ask for in prayer, believe that you have received it, and it will be yours."* You must first desire, long for, and then ask.

The confession of our mouths in prayer and intercession must be accompanied by a genuine heartfelt passion for what we are praying for. Psalm 145:18-19 says: *"The Lord is near to all who call on him... He fulfills the desires of those who fear him..."*. Love is the most powerful force of influence that exists. 1 Corinthians 13:8 says, *"Love never fails. But where there are prophecies, they will cease; where there are tongues, they will be stilled; where there is knowledge, it will pass away."* You cannot influence something you do not love. Influence is power to produce effects by intangible means. The key that God uses to influence humanity is love.

> *For God so loved the world that he gave his one and only Son, that whoever believes in him shall not perish but have eternal life. – John 3:16*

How does faith work?

Faith works through love, through the supernatural love of God.

The Amplified Bible says, "... The earnest (heartfelt, continued) prayer of a righteous man makes tremendous power available [dynamic in its working]" (James 5:16 AMPC)

Through the prayer of a passionate faith, the will of God is established on earth. This type of prayer will produce the desired results and will have a strong effect on the soul, the conscience, the way of thinking and the beliefs of the people for whom we pray. Your prayers will have great influence! If you continue to struggle on a natural level only, you will not see results, but if you take –by faith, the power and authority that God has already given you in the name of Jesus and pray passionately, you will open the heavens and you will see changes all around you.

When you pray with conviction (faith) and with passion (with all your heart), it inflames the wheel of creation. God wants to express the passion He has for His creation through our mouths. First, we must receive the heart of God and His passion for what we are praying, and then we can decree, pray, intercede and be the mouth of God here on earth, because out of the abundance of the heart speaks the mouth.

If you have asked yourself why the confession of your prayers have not worked, it may be that the lack of power in your prayers is the result of not having developed the passion in your heart needed to establish what you have been confessing. God Himself exercises this principle, before He establishes something, He desires it; He feels passion for what He confesses before confessing it, and then He establishes it. Psalm 115:3 says, "Our God is in heaven; he does whatever pleases him". The word desired, means having a move in the heart that leads you to act, it means to find pleasure in it. We must ask the Lord to give us passion for what we are going to pray for, before we begin to intercede.

How is power unlocked?

Power is unlocked when we activate the angels by speaking the Word of God.

Bless theLord, you His angels, Mighty in strength, who perform His word, obeying the voice of His word!
– *Psalm 103:20* NASB

For he will command his angels concerning you to guard you in all your ways. – *Psalm 91:11*

With the name of Jesus and the word of God in our mouths, we can activate the angels that have been set by God to work together with us. We can activate the liberating angels, ministering, and warriors who are mighty in strength, because they watch over us and strengthen us according to our needs.

You can start to experience the power of God's eternal life that is in you today, by knowing and loving God, by having a pure heart, by maturing spiritually, and by being willing to fight as you renew your mind. By God's grace, you can personally have experiences with God's type of life, and also be an instrument in God's hands to manifest His eternal life to others.

Chapter 3

God Is Your Portion and Your Inheritance

God's promise to every believer who reverently fears Him is: *"...you will be my people and I will be **your** God."* (Jeremiah 30:22). God has given Himself to us. There is no greater gift a person can receive. In God's kingdom's economy, the most valuable thing that exists is God Himself. The Lord told Aaron in Numbers 18:20, *"The Lord said to Aaron, 'You will have no inheritance in their land, nor will you have any share among them; I am your share and your inheritance among the Israelites.'"* Some may consider that receiving God as their portion or inheritance instead of lands is being shortchanged. But, whoever thinks this way, lacks revelation of who God is. The inheritance Aaron was receiving was the greatest portion, it was God Himself. We have the same inheritance today.

When God tells us that He is our God, He is saying He is making Himself available to us today in all His glory, and that we can have all that He is now and every day, as we appropriate ourselves of it by faith. God is supernatural, omnipotent, self-existing, self-sufficient, eternal, omnipresent, almighty, immutable, sovereign, infinite, holy, just, merciful, gracious etc., and all of this is at our disposition. The Lord told Abraham *"...Do not be afraid, Abram. I am your shield, your very great reward. I am your shield, and your exceedingly great reward"* (Genesis 15:1). With this He was telling Abraham that He was giving him the source of all blessings. You can tap into and receive your inheritance of who God is today. There are angels that are ministering spirits, but they are not your reward. Your reward is God, creator of heaven and earth (Psalm 146:6). What a large possession we have been given!

Our imperishable inheritance

We have an imperishable inheritance set aside for us, *"Blessed [gratefully praised and adored] be the God and Father of our Lord Jesus Christ, who according to His abundant and boundless mercy has caused us to be born again [that is, to be reborn from above- spiritually transformed, renewed, and set apart for His purpose] to an ever-living hope and confident assurance through the resurrection of Jesus Christ from the dead, [born anew] into an inheritance which is imperishable [beyond the reach of change] and undefiled and unfading, reserved in heaven for you."* 1 Peter 1:3-4 (AMPC)

We must recognize that none of us deserve such an inheritance; it is a gift through grace, that is received by faith. Through this provision, our spirit and our soul can be drenched and satisfied in everything that God is.

Unfortunately, many Christians are unaware of their God given inheritance and therefore have limited themselves from receiving the blessings they rightfully are entitled to receive. They are acting much like the prodigal son's brother who, even though he had a right to everything in his father's house, he never partook of any of it. (Luke 15:28-31) What we have in Christ is enough to fill and satisfy us on every level. If we have revelation of the value, the excellence and worth of what has been given to us, we will not lack anything ever again, because we have been graciously given the greatest gift and the biggest treasure. Those that reverentially fear and love God, find all they need in Him.

What can the world or Satan offer us that we cannot receive from our inheritance in God? In the gospels, we read that Satan tried to offer Jesus the world and its kingdoms if He would worship him. (Matthew 4 and Luke 4). What Satan did not realize was that Jesus knew the vast difference between what Satan offered Him and what he already had, which was God the Father, as His possession. It was evident to Jesus that what he already had was infinitely greater to what Satan offered Him. There was no comparison between the two.

God is my inheritance and my portion

If we were to ask King David what he found in having a close personal relationship with God, he would refer us to the many times he wrote about the communion he had with God as being worth much more than having kingdoms, jewels and fame, and how he considered God his inheritance and his portion:

Lord, you alone are my **portion** *and my cup; you make my lot secure. – Psalm 16:5*

My flesh and my heart may fail, but God is the strength of my heart and my **portion** *forever. – Psalm 73:26*

I cry to you, LORD; I say, "You are my refuge, my **portion** *in the land of the living." – Psalm 142:5*

King David referred to God as **his** God: *"And David said to Solomon: "My son, I had it in my heart to build a house for the Name of the Lord my God."* (1 Chronicles 22:7)

Also, note what prophet Jeremiah said about God being the portion of Jacob, the patriarch, symbol of his people: *"He who is the portion of Jacob is not like these (graven images), for he is the Maker of all things, including the people of his inheritance - the LORD Almighty is his name."* (Jeremiah 51:19)

Our Heavenly Father has assured an inheritance to us that we can enjoy here and now. *"Now if we are children, then we are heirs - heirs of God and co-heirs with Christ, if indeed we share in his sufferings in order that we may also share in his glory"* (Romans 8:17). This heavenly heritage is God's purpose and will for our lives.

The Scriptures describe God as the Almighty, (Genesis 17:1) El Shaddai, which means *the all-sufficient one.* Therefore, as your spirit and your soul are drenched in God through personal times of communion with Him, you will truly lack nothing! As you draw close to Him, you will be partaking of God's likeness, you will be filled with God Himself. It has always been and continues to be the will of God to pour out His love upon us, as we reverentially acknowledge who He is.

> *And hope does not put us to shame, because God's love has been poured out into our hearts through the Holy Spirit, who has been given to us. – Romans 5:5*

Since God has approached mankind with His love, He requires that we respond to Him also with love and draw close in fellowship with Him.

The greatest commandment in the Kingdom

God longs for a personal relationship with us. As a matter of fact, in Matthew 22:36-40 we read that our personal relationship with Him is the greatest commandment in His kingdom. However, a religious spirit that is evident in religious Christianity has conditioned people to be indifferent, apathetic and cold towards God. Many Christians have an intellectual type of relationship with the Lord, and they rationalize away the need to be close to God, and consider seeking God on a consistent basis to be fanatical. Countless christians have been corrupted by this religious spirit and because of it, they have withdrawn themselves from God.

In our society, it is now normal to be apathetic to God. We are living in a generation of desensitized people and we have been greatly affected by it. For many it is normal to be indifferent to God, people have become hard-hearted and callous. A hardened heart cannot feel the presence of God. When we lose our love and passion for God, all we have is a religion.

Where are you in your relationship with God? Would you describe your relationship with Him as passionate? Or has it grown cold and you have become insensitive to God's presence? Have you been cherishing the gift that God is in your life, or have you devalued Him?

Many reading this book have found it hard to shake off the religious spirit and religious mindset that they grew up with. However, as you read this book, God is giving you an opportunity to be set free. Before we continue, I would like to lead you to renounce to all religious spirits that may be restricting your ability to have a close and personal relationship with your heavenly Father.

Pray the following prayer out loud

Father God, I repent for replacing Your love with empty, void religious actions. I renounce the spirits of religion that have bound and restricted me from sincerely worshiping and praising You, that have kept me from a close relationship with You as my loving heavenly Father. I renounce every religious, pharisaic spirit that had a right to manipulate my soul and heart and restrict my ability to freely give myself to You.

Father God, forgive me for having allowed religion and

religious prayers to replace having a true relationship with You. I break all covenants with religious practices that I have made. I break all covenants with false religions! I break all covenants with religious traditions I learned from my past generations. I break all covenants with religious Christianity that does not allow me to freely worship You. I am set free in the name of Jesus.

Forgive me, Father God, for not having loved You the way You command in your Word. I repent from having lost my first love for You and for being indifferent to You. I make a covenant today to restore our relationship and rebuild my prayer altar daily. I renounce now and will continually renounce the obstacles that stop me from drawing close to You: If the obstacle has been unforgiveness towards others, I forgive every person who has offended me. (Mention each offense and confess forgiveness).

If the obstacle has been a hidden sin, I repent. (Confess each sin and repent wholeheartedly). If I have put other things before You, I decide now to remove them and give You priority in my life!

Father God, may I not be like the older brother of the prodigal son, who had everything at his disposition in the father's house but did not appropriate himself of it, and did not receive, nor activate his inheritance. I will enjoy and partake today of the good things You have already given me. I value and cherish what You have said, that You are my portion and my inheritance. I enjoy my inheritance and I receive it. There is no waiting in the Kingdom, everything is now, therefore, I receive You as my inheritance and today I encounter You!

Allow me to pray for you

Father God, in the name of Jesus Christ, I rebuke and cast out every spirit of religion from your people now reading this book. I declare that the spirit of religion comes out from within their bones and from within the marrow of their bones, from within their souls, from their conscious and subconscious minds and from anywhere else it may have had a right to attach itself to and remain in them. I deliver Your people, Father, in the name of Jesus, and undo every legal right that was allowed by their past generations. Generational curses of religion cannot remain in their lives because they have cried out to You to be set free, and You are faithful and powerful to set them free today. In Jesus' name, Amen!

In addition to religious spirits, and religious Christianity that have hindered many from a close relationship with God, the devil is an expert at attacking the time God's people separate to be in communion, prayer and intimacy with Him. We cannot allow anything to interfere and rob our attention when we seek God. If, when you go to pray, you spend thirty minutes out of your prayer time hour answering text messages, and in the next thirty minutes you get four interruptions, you will not achieve intimacy with God. Why do so many distractions continually pop up when we decide to be in God's presence and worship Him? Because the devil knows that if you get to a place of intimacy and fellowship with God, you will come out of that encounter full of His power. Be aware of Satan's plan to distract you every time you set your heart to seek God, so that you can overcome every obstacle.

What is fellowship with God and how do we obtain it?

Fellowship is sharing together and being in communion with God. Through fellowship with God, you can get to a place where you become one with Him. When you pray with all your heart, you can feel when true communion, (common union), is established with God. You will experience and know when you have become one with Him because you will feel something in your spirit. You will feel a shift, a peace, God's presence will become tangible to you and you will receive a sense of rest you did not have before you prayed. The more we are in His presence, the more of His love He can pour into us. His agape love is supernatural and no human being can obtain it unless they receive it from God.

God has given Himself to us. *Why is it so difficult for us to receive what He has already freely given us?* One of the main reasons is that we tend to believe that we have to struggle to get things, and therefore do not know how to *simply receive* them. To get is to obtain by struggle and effort. Getting things puts the burden on us, because we have to figure out how to manipulate the circumstances so that they work out the way we want them to. However, when it comes to the free gifts of God that He has already given us, the Bible talks about receiving, not getting. We receive by grace through faith, not through works. This Biblical principle is difficult for many people to grasp, because we have been taught by society, and the world we live in, that we have to always work for what we get. However, to receive is to experience freely. If obtaining what God has already freely given us would be a struggle and require effort, it would not be a free gift. One of the most devastating failures in religious Christianity is the inability to continuously receive what God has already freely given us.

> *On the last and greatest day of the festival, Jesus stood and said in a loud voice, "Let anyone who is thirsty come to me and drink." – John 7:37*

In the above Bible verse it says that *"anyone who is thirsty come to me and drink."* Therefore, the first corresponding action we must take is to come to Him and receive or drink. Nothing is mentioned here about earning or meriting this water. Anyone who knows he or she is thirsty is invited to come and drink. The second corresponding action or response we must make according to this Bible verse, is to acknowledge that our spirit and our soul were made to live from the living water of God. It is clear Jesus was not talking about physical thirst in these verses; what He is saying is that the soul has something that is similar to physical thirst. Your body was made to live on water. Your soul was made to live off God. It is important that you know that you were made to live off God. When you go without drinking natural water, your body gets thirsty. In the same way, the soul, when it goes without God, gets thirsty.

We are spiritually dehydrated and we don't know it

You have a soul and are a spirit. God created us human beings as a spirit that has a soul and lives in a body (see 1 Thessalonians 5:23). This means that two thirds of our being are immaterial and spiritual, the spirit and the soul, and therefore only a relationship with God, Who is a spirit, can truly make us whole. There is a "you" that is more than your body, and if it does not drink from the greatness, wisdom, power, goodness, justice, holiness and love of God (that can only be obtained when we are in His presence), it will slowly die of thirst. We can be spiritually dehydrated and not know it, just as we can be dehydrated in the natural and not be aware of it. Doctors say that when we drink less water than our body requires, the imbalance can lead to serious health problems because water is crucial for our organs to function properly. Even becoming mildly dehydrated can seriously impact our body's ability to function. Doctors also say that by the time we feel thirsty, we are already mildly dehydrated. In other words, you can be dehydrated right now and not know it, because you do not feel great thirst. In the natural, it is recommended that we drink enough water so that we never reach the point where we feel thirsty, in other words, we should not wait until we are feeling parched, and then drink enough water to quench our thirst. We should drink water regularly. Similarly, you cannot allow your soul and your spirit to be out of the presence of God long enough to be parched and dry spiritually; you should drink of Jesus regularly.

Many of God's people are living completely dry in the spirit. They live as if they are in a spiritual desert where there is no source of water and they are at a point of spiritual dehydration. God wants to lead you to the wells of living waters to satisfy your thirst and to renew your strength. Listen to what the Lord says in Psalm 23:2-3, 5 "He makes me lie down in green pastures, he leads me beside quiet waters, he refreshes my soul. He guides me along the right paths for his name's sake [...] You anoint my head with oil; my cup overflows." God is saying to you: "Come and drink, come and satisfy your soul." God will pour Himself upon you and will refresh and strengthen you as you abide in His presence.

Jesus is what our souls' need

Jesus does not have what our souls need; He is what our souls' need. Jesus is what we drink because He said, "Come to me and drink." He is the living water. Our souls were created to be continuously drenched with the presence of our Lord. The emptiness in our hearts is really a lack of Jesus. This is how the soul lives: it lives on Jesus. It is revived as it drinks Jesus. This drinking is not something you do with your mouth, you do it with your soul, and you do it spiritually. You cannot finish reading this book and remain thirsty and dry! You bought this book so that you could encounter God and drink of Him!

"He that believeth on me, as the scripture hath said, out of his belly shall flow rivers of living water" (John 7:38 KJV). The belly is the inner being, (whether we call it belly, heart, soul or spirit, it is from our inner being that rivers of living water will flow). What does it mean for rivers to flow from your inner man? It means that when you come to Jesus to drink, you do not just

get a single drink, but you get a spring, and a fountain. You will never have to search again for a source of satisfaction for your soul anywhere else! Joy, peace and security for your soul will flow from Jesus. There is an experience, an encounter, a baptism of the Spirit that we can have; a continuous fellowship with the Spirit of the Living God that will continuously satisfy us. It is for everyone who believes. Receive, simply receive; you do not have to struggle to get it. It has been freely given to you! Break that tough exterior, that shield you have placed over your heart, and allow God's presence to flood your heart as you worship Him.

∞∞∞∞∞∞∞

Your encounter with God is not just for you to feel good, it is for you to spread the power of God's supernatural love to others.

∞∞∞∞∞∞∞

God is calling you to drink from Him, and then to be a fountain of living water for others. You will become a fountain of water for others to drink from. Jesus said *"But whoever drinks the water that I give him will never be thirsty again. But the water that I give him will become in him a spring of water [satisfying **his thirst for God**] welling up [continually flowing, bubbling within him] to eternal life."* (John 4:14 - AMP)

As I was writing this book, God impressed upon me to activate you, so that once you drink from Him, and once you are satisfied, you could become fountains of living water for others to drink from. Therefore, I invite you to make the following commitment to the Lord; say it out loud: "Father in the name of Jesus I desire to take Your living water and supernatural love wherever I go. I will take the good news of the gospel of Your kingdom and make it known to others so that they can also enjoy You, God, as their portion and their inheritance".

Dear reader, I will commission you right now to go and find those people who are dying of thirst, and give them to drink:

> *Father in the name of Jesus, I commission the readers of this book to be fountains of living water and manifest the power of the kingdom of God. I declare that they are carriers of the supernatural power of God's love wherever they go, and that they reach those that surround them for Your kingdom! I commission Your people to go and release the supernatural power of Your love wherever they go, to evangelize, to heal the sick, and to deliver the oppressed. Freely they have received, and freely they will give, with great manifestations of your Spirit.*

Chapter 4

Seeking God Through Praise and Worship

We can seek God every day through praise and worship. Praise is to proclaim who God is. It is when we brag about Him. It is when we magnify His name and we focus on His greatness. It is to declare His mighty works, exalt Him and invite others to do the same, like King David did in Psalm 34:3 *"Glorify the Lord with me; let us exalt his name together."* Praise summons The King to come and appear. It is the procession of the King. We must know that God is God to be able to praise Him properly.

Worship is different. It is to bow down and kiss God's hand. It is an inner attitude of the heart, full of humility, respect and reverence expressed by the posture of our body. Worship provokes God to reveal Himself. Worship is the coronation of The King. Our worship sets the atmosphere for miracles to manifest and for God to speak. If you ever want God to move in your circumstances, you must worship Him. We can see an example of the power of worship in the story of the Canaanite woman, who had a demonically oppressed daughter (see Matthew 15:21-28). Once she realized that everything else she did to try to get Jesus' attention failed, she instinctively worshipped Him. When she worshipped Jesus, He acknowledged her request and performed the miracle she was asking for.

Praise and worship will cause God to draw closer to us, and as He draws closer, He will manifest His presence and all that He is. In the Scriptures, we see how worship affected God and, at the same time, how it affected those who worshipped Him.

David fervently praised and worshiped God

David's heart was revealed in the book of Psalms, by two prevalent thoughts expressed throughout each verse he wrote. These two thoughts are: dependence on God, and heartfelt worship. David learned that worship not only pleased and affected God's heart, he learned that worship also affected his own heart and his desires. He stated: *"One thing I ask from the Lord, this only do I seek: that I may dwell in the house of the Lord all the days of my life, to gaze on the beauty of the Lord and to seek him in his temple"* (Psalm 27:4).

When we passionately worship Him, His heart opens to receive our worship and at the same time, our hearts open to receive His love. King David passionately sought God. He wanted to know Him and to be in His presence. He desired to please Him. He wanted to see God, and he sought Him continuously. He proclaimed: *"You, God, are my God, earnestly I seek you; I thirst for you, my whole being longs for you, in a dry and parched land where there is no water. I have seen you in the sanctuary and beheld your power and your glory [...] On my bed I remember you; I think of you through the watches of the night"* (Psalm 63:1-2, 6). It is evident by these Bible references, that David loved God and depended on his relationship with God for everything.

Because of his passionate pursuit of God, King David received revelation of the importance of living in the presence of God. We too must receive this revelation, because there is one essential ingredient needed to sustain the Christian life, and that is to live in God's presence. We have a continual need and are totally dependent on Him because He created us and He is our source. God's presence should not be a place we visit, but the place where we live. "For in Him we live and move and have our being..." (Acts 17:28). Every day, the first thing we should do is seek God's presence through praise and worship because the first and most fundamental thing necessary to truly be effective in life, is to remain continuously connected with Him. There is always more of God for us to know, more to desire, more to love. The problem we have is that many times we are not as hungry for God as David was. We have little of the presence of God in many christian circles today because we lack a desire for Him.

Why do we worship God?

Do you only worship God for what He has done for you or for what He can do for you? Change that motivation and worship Him for who He is. Your passionate worship of Him will lead you into intimacy with Him. Do not be afraid to get closer to God. A true worshipper approaches God with confidence because of the revelation they have regarding God's deep love for them.

If we claim to love the Lord, we will not be content being away from His presence for long periods of time. That is why God, in His infinite wisdom, created us as a spirit. We are a spirit, we have a soul and we live in a body (see 1 Thessalonians 5:23). It is with our spirit that we can be in constant communion with the Holy Spirit at any moment of our day, especially whenever we notice we have been overly distracted from Him with daily cares. We can recall our soul –mind, will and emotions– to God wherever we are, and especially whenever we get over-burdened and anxious. You can offer your heart to God every moment of the day by simply praising Him for an instant and asking Him for His grace.

You can show Him you love Him at any given moment, by turning your mind towards Him. We can do this any time on any day, and not just on special occasions, such as Sundays, or Easter or Thanksgiving Day, or when we pray in the mornings before we leave our homes. We can become more aware of God's presence and experience His glory whenever we desire and wherever we go. We can make our hearts an altar wherever we are, by taking fragments of time to acknowledge and be aware of His presence by talking with Him, ministering to Him privately and allowing Him to minister to us.

At will, throughout the day, we can momentarily withdraw with Him by recalling our mind to Him with worship, expressing our affection towards Him and declaring our faith in Him. At these times, we can say something as simple as: "Lord, I acknowledge that Your presence is with me right now because You are omnipresent. I receive Your grace right now to do what I cannot do in my own strength." At that moment tell Him whatever is in your heart. You should be able to say with all sincerity: "Jesus, You are all I need. I trust You with everything I am and everything I have."

Our relationship with God leads us to trust Him

In his book entitled: *Daily Encounters with God*, Apostle Guillermo Maldonado states: "Trust is a spiritual element that is born in the heart and is based on a relationship, where both parties know each other intimately... Trust represents our 'walk' with God, and the way we love, obey and live for Him... When we trust in God, we rest assured; confident in His character, integrity and faithfulness... Many are strong in their faith, but weak in their trust. The more intimate your relationship is with God, the more your faith will increase."

We cannot underestimate the importance of believing in the power that is released when we trust God and rely solely on His grace. If we are to truly worship God, we must have hearts filled with faith and trust in God and His unfailing grace. Many times, we try to control or manipulate the circumstances that surround us, instead of simply exercising faith in God's grace, strength and ability to do what we cannot do in our own strength. There are many things that can only be obtained by grace through faith, including our salvation (Ephesians 2:8).

When our prayers are not faith based prayers resting in God's grace, they become manipulative prayers. We try to get things done and set things in order by using natural means. However, in the long run, we realize that all our efforts are of no effect. If we truly want to walk in faith and be able to freely worship God from a heart that trusts in Him, we need to cease our striving.

We need to just shut our mouths and stop trying to straighten out things on our own and instead get to know God, who sits sovereignly on His throne. We will be in awe of what God can do without us manipulating the circumstances. For many christians, it is difficult to understand God's grace. They think they must be doing something all the time, when in fact God wants us to rest on Him. There are many things that come only from the Father's throne of mercy, if we just apply faith in His grace. Allow God to show Himself to be God. Our responsibility is simply to trust, apply faith, and stop relying on our own strength. Let go and let God. God is telling you personally today: *"...Be still and know that I am God..."* (Psalm 46:10). In other words, cease your striving and worship Him. As we trust God and rely on His grace, we are truly worshipping Him. God seeks and desires this type of worship.

Worship leads us to encounter God

Worship shuts down the soul –mind, will and emotions– and it is then that we are able to go into the Holy of Holies where we can encounter our Lord, where He manifests and becomes real to us. The moment we yield our heart, mind and will to the Lord, we experience a type of death to self, and that is when we become a living sacrifice, acceptable to God.

Why be satisfied with just a brief moment of worship? We are content with too little of God. He has infinite treasures to give us. However, if we devote only a meager amount of time to prayer and praise and worship, we restrain the flow of God's abundant grace towards us. If God can find a soul filled with a lively faith and desire for Him, He will pour His grace into it. Do not stop God's flood of grace in your life because of your lack of abundant honor through praise and worship.

Worship brings the presence of God. His presence is what nourishes us, keeps us and transforms us into the image of Christ Jesus. We need revelation from the Holy Spirit to know how to worship God as He should be worshipped, so that God's presence not only comes and hovers over us for a brief moment, but that it remains, settles, and abides with us continuously.

Spending hours with God is the best investment of our time

One of the expressions of love is the dedication of time. Invest yourself every day by dedicating time to praise and worship God. Time is a portion, or fragment, of your life. Spend your life on God. Be occupied with Him. To be occupied means to be used, busy and active with something. In other words, on the door of your prayer room there should be a sign that says: "Do Not Disturb, I Am Busy with God."

Spend yourself on God with the conviction and expectation that you will achieve something wondrous. Use all your resources, your strength and your energy on God. You may spend long periods of time just saying: "I love You, I desire You, I need You, my soul cries out for You. Thank You, give me more of You Lord, I desire Your presence. You are Holy and I want to see You! Manifest Your presence! My God, I am all Yours, do what You will with me. I am Yours and You are mine. May Your name be lifted up, may Your name be exalted!" and other such expressions.

What will you have been doing during this time? You would have been expressing your passion for God, your need of Him and your love for Him. You would have said as King David said: *"Do not cast me from your presence or take your Holy Spirit from me."* (Psalm 51:11).

What is the result of our investment?

You will become experienced in God, because what you invest time in, you become proficient in. You will have experiences with God, you will sharpen your spiritual ear to hear His voice and you will be able to bring God's presence wherever you go. You will know Him because He will reveal Himself to you and you will start to comprehend His Word and His faithfulness!

You will become that which you invest your time in. Become like God. When you invest your time in praising and worshipping God, what is His, becomes yours. As a result of our close relationship with God, His attributes will be poured out on us: wisdom, power, knowledge, might, insight and revelation. Our hearts will beat as one with God's heart. What one loves, the other one loves. God's anointing, grace and favor will be poured out upon us.

True worship honors God

There is no such thing as being able to deeply worship God and at the same time be in rebellion and sin. If we are in rebellion (if we are full of unconfessed sin), God will reject our worship. King David, who had a heart after God's own heart, realized this, and therefore he was quick to repent from sin.

If your lifestyle does not express the beauty of holiness through an extravagant love for God, and you do not desire to be in submission to Him, your worship will not be true worship. Your obedience to God will always determine the density and deepness of your worship to Him. In other words, worship did not begin when you first opened your mouth to say "Holy." True worship started when you started to obey God five, ten, fifteen days, months or even years ago.

The words we speak come from the heart, from who we are, *"For as he [a man] thinks in his heart, so is he"* (Proverbs 23:7 nkjv). If we speak words of worship to God, but have disobeyed Him without repentance, or do not sincerely love Him, He does not accept our worship. That is why in some congregations the worship is light, and the presence of God is not felt, because those present do not truly have a lifestyle of extravagant love and extreme obedience towards God. The thoughts of the corrupt and disobedient hearts of men make their worship unacceptable to God. When there is a combination of worship with the lips and disobedience in the heart, the worship is corrupted. However, if we humble ourselves, repent of all disobedience and seek God, He will transform our hearts. If you want to be a true worshiper, you must first be willing to fully obey God because true worship is contingent on our obedience to Him. Cheap worship is to honor God merely with our lips and not with our actions. Look at what God's Word says:

> *You hypocrites! Isaiah was right when he prophesied about you: "These people honor me with their lips, but their hearts are far from me. They worship me in vain; their teachings are merely human rules." Jesus called the crowd to him and said, "Listen and understand. What goes into someone's mouth does not defile them, but what comes out of their mouth, that is what defiles them." – Matthew 15:7-11*

In this verse, the word defile means to render profane, unhallowed or unacceptable to God. When there is corporate or individual worship that comes from sincere obedient hearts, unplanned God encounters will occur, both in a corporate setting and in people's personal lives. A service filled with sincere heartfelt worship will be charged with the presence of God.

Sincerely examine Your heart

Before you worship God, examine your heart and look to see if you have been disobedient to Him. If your heart is in that condition, repent and seek God's forgiveness. If you seek Him with sincerity, you will find Him. As you seek Him, you will hear His voice. Our part is to repent full-heartedly. It is then that God's supernatural grace can transform us. Our hearts must be in good standing with God to be able to experience and enjoy the results of sincere praise and worship. What is God after? He is looking for those who are sensitive to Him and obedient to His word. If we are quick to repent from all sin, and recognize that we have offended Him, He will forgive us. He sees our heart. *"Whoever conceals their sins does not prosper, but the one who confesses and renounces them finds mercy"* (Proverbs 28:13).

When we worship God with extravagant love and extreme submission, God will manifest His presence where we are. God will show up as He did in the book of Acts when Paul and Silas were in jail, not for doing something wrong, but because they had been doing God's will. They had set a slave girl free from a spirit of divination. While in jail they did not despair, instead they worshipped God and God appeared!

> *After they had been severely flogged, they were thrown into prison, and the jailer was commanded to guard them carefully. When he received these orders, he put them in the inner cell and fastened their feet in the stocks. About midnight Paul and Silas were praying and singing hymns to God, and the other prisoners were listening to them. Suddenly there was such a violent earthquake that the foundations of the prison were shaken. At once all the prison doors flew open, and everyone's chains came loose.*
> *– Acts 16:23-26*

We must make a throne with our worship for God's presence to descend upon it. God is seeking those that worship in spirit and in truth, to show Himself mighty. The Spirit of God leads us to be worshipers. True worship will cause His presence to be tangible and His great power will manifest. At the moment when you reach deep worship, the King of Kings arrives to meet with you. At these moments, do not get distracted, remain anticipating and expectant, attentive and reverent towards God and He will reveal Himself in a greater way to you.

What does God desire? What brings joy to Him? What will make His presence manifest? What pleases Him? The answer to these questions is: our deep desire to have an intimate relationship with Him! Intimacy is the place where you open your heart to God and He opens His heart to you. That is the place where God manifests His plans and purposes to you and you conceive His mindset. Conception takes place when you worship God, giving Him your complete undivided attention.

Intimacy is the place where we conceive new things from God

Where there is no worship there is no intimacy. Both in the natural and in the spiritual world, where there is no intimacy, there is no pregnancy. A large majority of believers never truly worship God, which means they never conceive anything new from God.

The consummation of marriage between a man and a woman is the sexual act; in the same way, the consummation of worship is the manifestation of God's presence. There is a moment when His presence comes. That is the sign that God is satisfied. With His presence, He is saying: I am satisfied. If His presence does not come, it is because you did not worship wholeheartedly, or you did not stay and wait long enough for it to descend. Keep pressing on! Keep pressing in worship, and also worship in tongues. The purpose of intimacy is procreation; to beget or bring forth something new from God.

How do we know we have reached intimacy with God?

You will know you have achieved intimacy with God because at that time, nothing else matters. When you reach intimacy with God, nothing else matters but Him; not your business, your family problems, etc. It is then that you will hear His voice clearly.

God desires great depths of intimacy with His people. He desires that we diligently seek Him, setting all distractions aside and focus on giving Him praise and worship. He desires us to be motivated exclusively by our deep love for Him, and that we seek Him continuously, and not only when we need Him to resolve some problem in our lives. As you do this, you will be coming into unity with God, you will become one with Him. From that unity comes everything we need. We seek Him and not His blessings, and as a result of our heartfelt desire for Him, He blesses us and empowers us.

Achieving this type of unity with God may take time, but its results are greatly worth the time and effort exerted. Therefore, take time to have communion with God. It is in this atmosphere that God commences to reveal Himself to us and we get to know Him and see Him face to face. It is in these times of deep worship that we conceive something supernatural from Him as Mary, the mother of Jesus, conceived of the Holy Spirit. We conceive our destiny, the salvation of our family and indefinite blessings.

Transformed by His Presence

There are many things that will be transformed in our lives as we worship God, and we will receive innumerable benefits as a result of our intimacy with Him. Worship will cause the following transformations in your life:

- **It will change you.** It is only in God's presence that we are changed. The length of time you are in God's presence determines the level of transformation of your heart to the heart of God. As children of God we do many things. We go to church, serve in the ministry, give offerings, and so on. However, none of these things change our hearts. The only thing that transforms us into the image of Christ is being in God's presence. Does that mean we do not have to go to church? Of course not, it is a command of God to congregate, because it is at church where you will learn to have communion with Him. If you attend a spirit filled church that praises and worships God extravagantly, you will have your first experiences with God's transforming power at that church. However, you should not stop merely with the experiences you have at church. You must build a personal altar for God of your own. A place where you meet with Him on a regular basis, not just on Sunday mornings.

- **It will empower you to believe.** As you have experiences with God, these experiences will strengthen your faith and you will be able to stand firm on God's truth in times of trials. No one will deter you from the truth because you had a personal one on one experience with the truth. *"Jesus answered, 'I am the way and the truth and the life. No* *one comes to the Father except through me."* (John 14:6). Throughout your life many people will express their own personal opinions and will try to persuade you to doubt God and His word. At those times, what will sustain you are the experiences you have had in intimacy with the truth that confirmed who God really is. In God's presence, the Holy Spirit empowers us to believe.

- **It will give you boldness.** *"...but the people who know their God shall be strong, and carry out great exploits but the people who know their God shall be strong, and carry out great exploits."* (Daniel 11:32 nkjv) God's presence creates a holy place for you to live in, separated from the mundane, charged with the power of God.

It is my desire that everyone that reads this book, will continually (daily), and practically practice the presence of God in their lives and make time to praise and worship Him. Remember, the purpose of praise and worship is to exalt God and for you to empty yourself and fill yourself with Him.

God is our end, our aim and our focus. When we pray, we should lose awareness of everything around us but God, and praise and bless Him with all our strength. God is intimately present within us!

Chapter 5

Passion

God has a message for you. It is written within every book of His Word. His message is: "I passionately love you." He does not want you to forget that He desires you above all else, before your service to Him, before your good deeds, before your hard work. Dear reader, please consider this eternal truth: God's love for you is passionate.

> *The Lord appeared...saying, "I have loved you with an everlasting love; I have drawn you with unfailing kindness."*
> *– Jeremiah 31:3*

It is the passion God has for the souls of men that caused Him to send His son Jesus to the world to die in our place.

> *This is how God showed his love among us: He sent His one and only Son into the world that we might live through Him. This is love: not that we loved God, but that He loved us and sent His Son as an atoning sacrifice for our sins.*
> *– 1 John 4:9-10*

Jesus' desire was to reveal to us the character of God the Father, so that we would be able to know and experience the same love He and His Father shared. *"I have made Your Name known to them and revealed Your character and Your very Self, and I will continue to make [You] known, that the love which You have bestowed upon Me may be in them [felt in their heart] and that I [Myself] may be in them"* (John 17:26 AMPC). That was Jesus' mission on earth, and that is the desire of God the Father for all humanity. It is that same passion that motivated Jesus to carry the cross on which He was crucified for our sins. It is because of that passion that he forgave those who put Him to death. As a matter of fact, if you look up the word passion in the dictionary, you will find that one of its definitions is: "the suffering and death of Jesus."

What is passion?

It is a force that drives a person to act, or drives a person towards that which they desire greatly. When you have passion for someone, you have a strong attachment, or feel a strong love for them, and are so hopelessly crazy in love that you pursue the object of your love fervently. Passion is a force that moves in God Himself.

What does God ask in return from us for His passionate love? God longs and desires our love. Our heart is what He desires, our passion for Him. *"My son, give me your heart and let your eyes delight in my ways"* (Proverbs 23:26). The thing God cares the most about is how much we love Him. Jesus asked Peter three times *"Do you love me?"* (John 21:17). God wants us to passionately love

Him. However, He does not force us to love Him, because love cannot be coerced or obligated. It has to be given freely. We have been given the choice to love God or not to love Him.

God wants you to really come to know, practically through experience, not by mere intellectual activity, but by the operation of the Holy Spirit, the love of Christ, as Paul prayed for in Ephesians 3:16-19, *"I pray that out of his glorious riches he may strengthen you with power through his Spirit in your inner being, so that Christ may dwell in your hearts through faith. And I pray that you, being rooted and established in love, may have power, together with all the Lord's holy people, to grasp how wide and long and high and deep is the love of Christ, and to know this love that surpasses knowledge—that you may be filled to the measure of all the fullness of God."*

The Ephesians that the Apostle Paul prayed for did not fully grasp God's love for them. If this is true of you, you need to prayerfully ask the Holy Spirit to reveal to you the wonders of God's mighty love.

Knowing the vast love of God

There was a time in my life when I did not comprehend God's infinite love for me, and one day while I prayed, the Holy Spirit gave me a vision about God's vast love. I believe this vision will help you grasp the immensity of the love of God. In the vision, I saw myself in a big beautiful field. The field was so large that I could not see any borders or where it ended. In this vision, I knew that I was standing in the exact center of the field. What was remarkable about it was that as I walked, no matter how far or fast I walked, I remained in the very center of the field, as if the center of the field itself always moved with me. Then I heard the voice of the Lord tell me: "This is how my love is for you; no matter where you walk, or how far you go, you will always be in the center of my love. It is so vast, you will never be able to walk out of it."

It is awesome to know that we are the beneficiaries of a love relationship with God the Father; the God of heaven and earth. We receive many blessings from this relationship, because of who He is, and because of His faithfulness.

God could have made us His slaves or just mere servants, and we still would have been blessed by serving Him. He could have made humanity robotic type of beings, but He chose to give us a free will to choose for ourselves to love Him. If we did not have the choice of free will, there would not be love in our hearts for God. Therefore, He allows us to choose. *So you are no longer a slave, but God's child; and since you are his child, God has made you also an heir* (Galatians 4:7).

See what great love the Father has lavished on us, that we should be called children of God! And that is what we are! – 1 John 3:1

Many Christians have not received the revelation of the love of God, and therefore live their lives as merely servants of God, and not as His beloved children. They are still bound to fear and feel rejected and inferior, even though God's perfect love casts out all fear! *"There is no fear in love. But perfect love drives out fear, because fear has to do with punishment. The one who fears is not made perfect in love"* (1 John 4:18).

God never wants to see our relationship with Him deteriorate. His love for us has never changed, but ours for Him has. He wants us to come back to Him, full of passionate love. Has your love for God grown cold?

When passion is lost

In the natural life, during a certain age, both men and women experience a decrease in passion, which is measured as sexual drive. During this time, there is a loss of sexual desire, and the married couple is unfruitful; they do not bear children. Similarly, those that have been walking with God for many years also tend to lose the ability to be passionate for God and they become unfruitful because they may feel they have too many problems, too many responsibilities, are too tired, and so on. However, God wants us to remain passionate for Him at all times.

There are good Christian people reading this book right now who at one point in their lives were passionate for God, but now they have lost that desire. I invite you to come back and have an encounter with the God that loves you! God's will is to manifest Himself to you now. The encounter you had with the Lord days ago, or weeks ago, is not enough. God has something to give you today.

It is time to leave everything behind and encounter the God

that loves you. The psalmist said: *"I trust in God's unfailing love for ever and ever"* (Psalm 52:8). *"Give thanks to the God of heaven. His love endures forever"* (Psalm 136:26).

> *"Even now," declares the Lord, "return to me with all your heart, with fasting and weeping and mourning." Rend your heart and not your garments. Return to the Lord your God, for he is gracious and compassionate, slow to anger and abounding in love... – Joel 2:12-13*

> *But you, Lord, are a compassionate and gracious God, slow to anger, abounding in love and faithfulness.*
> *– Psalm 86:15*

> *But I am like an olive tree flourishing in the house of God; I trust in God's unfailing love for ever and ever. – Psalm 52:8*

> *The Lord your God is with you, the Mighty Warrior who saves. He will take great delight in you; in his love he will no longer rebuke you, but will rejoice over you with singing. – Zephaniah 3:17*

> *Your love, Lord, reaches to the heavens, your faithfulness to the skies. – Psalm 36:5*

> *How priceless is your unfailing love, O God! People take refuge in the shadow of your wings. – Psalm 36:7*

Created for love

We were created to experience God's love and we were created to love Him above all else. (See Mark 12:30). Per God's Word, the greatest commandment is to have passionate love for Him. Therefore, in the eyes of God, our extreme desire, or love for anything else is an offense to Him. For us to have the type of fervent love for God that He commands us to have, a love that is above all else, we need to regularly search and scrutinize our hearts (our motives, our deepest desires) and be willing to repent and cleanse it from every other rival that may have taken the place that belongs only to Him.

In Revelation 2:2, 4-5 we read the letter addressed to the Church in Ephesus. Jesus says: *"I know your deeds [...] Yet I hold this against you: You have forsaken the love you had at first... Repent and do the things you did at first. If you do not repent, I will come to you and remove your lampstand from its place."* Forsaking the first love for God means losing the excitement of loving and knowing Him. In Revelation 3:15-16, in the letter to the church at Laodicea, Jesus says: *"I know your deeds, that you are neither cold nor hot. I wish you were either one or the other! So, because you are lukewarm —neither hot nor cold— I am about to spit you out of my mouth."* Satan is after our love for God and wants to destroy it. The lack of love for God is a sign of the end of the times.

Jesus said some people hear the Word of God, and a desire for God is awakened in their hearts but then, *"as they go on their way they are choked by life's worries, riches and pleasures, and they do not mature"*, (Luke 8:14). He also said that, *"the worries of this life, the deceitfulness of wealth and the desires for other things come in and choke the word, making it unfruitful"* (Mark 4:19). It is important to note that "the pleasures" of life and "the desires for other things" mentioned in the above Bible verses are not evil things in and of themselves. These are not vices. They are our love for gardening, decorating, traveling, hobbies, work, TV watching, internet surfing, social media, shopping, exercising, cooking, talking on the phone, etc. However, these pleasures of life over time can become deadly substitutes for God in our hearts, to the extent that we spend more time doing those things rather than using that time to seek God. Innocent pleasures can easily lure us away from the narrow path of seeking God.

Fasting keeps our love for God fervent

One of the weapons we can use to make sure we do not veer off the path of having a passionate relationship with God is dedicating time to prayer and fasting. By fasting we can declare an inward war with our own appetites that compete with our hunger for God. The Apostle Paul said, *"For [His] sake I have lost all things. I consider them garbage, that I may gain Christ"* (Philippians 3:8).

There is spiritual delight to be found in God that far supersedes anything this physical world has to offer. It is impossible for anyone to live in the presence of the living God, the Maker of heaven and earth, and still be looking for something better on this earth to satisfy them. Unfortunately, we often trade being in the presence of our heavenly Father for temporal things; but these things will never be able to truly meet the expectations and needs of our soul. It is for this reason, and vital for our spiritual well-being, that we periodically scrutinize and search our heart in order to cleanse it of any rival to God. Once you detect what has been robbing your affection for God, you must choose to sacrifice it and let it go to regain your passion for God.

A perfect example of God's demand that we have nothing consume our love and attention other than Him, is found in the example of Abraham in Genesis 22:2. In this passage God asked Abraham to sacrifice Isaac, his son. Why would God call for such a sacrifice? Because it was a test. The question put to the test was, did Abraham delight in the fear of the Lord more than he delighted in his own son? God did not ask Abraham to sacrifice Isaac because Isaac was evil. On the contrary, it was because, in Abraham's eyes, he seemed indispensable for the fulfillment of God's promise, and because Abraham loved Isaac deeply.

When Abraham stretched out his hand to kill his son and the heir of God's promise, *"...the angel of the Lord called out to him from heaven, 'Abraham! Abraham!' 'Here I am,' he replied. 'Do not lay a hand on the boy,' he said. 'Do not do anything to him. Now I know that you fear God, because you have not withheld from me your son, your only son.'"* (Genesis 22:11-12).

God's will for each one of us is that we prefer Him over all things, and to practice that preference every day in our lives.

We can say with our mouths that we prefer God over all other things, but, do we really practice what we say? God wants you to have fresh testimonies of your own acts of actual preference of Him over His gifts, which is why He invites you to pray and fast. He invites you to separate yourself from those things which consume you, and seek Him through prayer.

We can easily deceive ourselves to think that we love God the way He commands us to, but the proof of our love needs to be frequently put to the test, and we must show God our preference for Him not merely with words, but with the actions of voluntary sacrifice. Many small acts of preferring fellowship with God above other things —such as eating, sleeping, working, spending time with your family or your favorite hobby— will form a habit of seeking God and having communion with Him, the One Who truly deserves our undivided attention and fervent passion.

Fasting keeps us from turning God's gifts into idols

Fasting is the voluntary abstinence from foods, and other pleasures of this world, to seek God and His presence, and to strengthen our relationship with Him. Fasting is the way by which you can say to God: More than I desire any pleasure in this world –including food– my soul desires You. As a result of correct fasting and praying, we will have encounters with God and will *"taste and see that the Lord is good..."* (Psalm 34:8), and the temporal things of this world will no longer appeal to us in the same way.

Fasting is an intensifier of spiritual desire, it fans the flames of hunger for God. The purpose of fasting and praying is to maintain or regain hunger, love, passion or homesickness for God (the love-sick pain for God we may have lost) and also to abide in communion with Him to hear His voice; for us to intently listen to Him.

Correct fasting includes scrutinizing our hearts to express sorrow and repentance for all our sins. If during the time you fast, you do not seek God and ask Him to show you every hidden sin that may be in your heart, you are not truly fasting. Many sins are subtle and hard to detect without the aid of the Holy Spirit, such as complaining, judging others, criticizing, pride, jealousy, rebellion, independence, greed, selfishness, manipulation, sowing discord between people instead of peace, bitterness, oppressing others, strife, quarreling, gossiping, fear, etc. If any of these things are within us, it is up to us to humble ourselves and ask the Holy Spirit to show them to us during our fast. If we are sincere, the Holy Spirit will let us know what is hidden within our hearts. Then our only option is to repent and allow God to change us, as we humbly recognize our heart's condition. David said, "I humbled my soul with fasting" (Psalm 35:13 kjv). If we fast with the correct motives and in the right way, we will be truly fulfilled and satisfied with the bountiful pleasures of God's love, because there is vast spiritual delight to be found in God alone.

> *"Even now," declares the Lord, "return to me with all your heart, with fasting and weeping and mourning." Rend your heart and not your garments. Return to the Lord your God, for he is gracious and compassionate, slow to anger and abounding in love, and he relents from sending calamity. – Joel 2:12-13*

Fasting realigns our hearts to God

Correct fasting and prayer will keep your relationship with God and love for Him fervent. Sadly, we have changed the purpose of fasting to make it mainly a means by which we can get something from God –an answer to a prayer– instead of it being primarily a means to draw closer to Him. By fasting, we put temporal things aside to obtain superior satisfaction in God. Fasting is a pain we should be willing to experience because we recognize our need of God and are lovesick for Him and truly hungry for His presence. As we do this, we will be able to say to the Lord with all honesty *"... earth has nothing I desire besides you"* (Psalm 73:25). Therefore, fasting should include abstinence from anything which is legitimate in and of itself, for the sake of pursuing God and His purposes. There are many activities we can choose to do, which are right and normal, and perfectly legitimate, but we can also choose to put them aside to seek something infinitely and eternally better: God Himself. That is what fasting is about.

The important thing in correct fasting is not only abstaining from food per se, but that we voluntarily put aside anything and everything that is, or has become, a substitute for God in our lives, and seek Him with all our hearts, mind, soul and strength. Therefore, in addition to food, you may also need to *fast* other things. Some things that may be fasted other than food may be: Watching a favorite television program on the night you normally watch it, and instead spend that time praying and listening to God, singing along with praise music and bowing down to worship Him, hearing (by listening intently) to an anointed preaching, or reading an anointed book. Also, instead of eating lunch, you can take the Bible to a quiet place and sit down for a spiritual meal. During this time expect to hear God speak to you. By doing this, what will you be doing? You will be seeking to realign your heart's affection towards God again, putting aside all the other things that normally consume your attention and affection.

Fasting is not only the forfeit of evil, it is also the voluntary forfeit of good things

Good things can subtly do great damage to our hearts and our relationship with God. An important revelation regarding fasting is that, we fast not only to forfeit evil, but also to voluntarily forfeit good things or the pleasures of life.

In the parable of the Great Banquet, God describes what keeps us from His love. Please notice that the list contains a piece of land, a yoke of oxen, and a wife:

> *When one of those at the table with him heard this, he said to Jesus, "Blessed is the one who will eat at the feast in the kingdom of God." Jesus replied: "A certain man was preparing a great banquet and invited many guests. At the time of the banquet he sent his servant to tell those who had been invited, 'Come, for everything is now ready.' "But they all alike began to make excuses. The first said, 'I have just bought a field, and I must go and see it. Please excuse me.' "Another said, 'I have just bought five yoke of oxen, and I'm on my way to try them out. Please excuse*

> me.' "Still another said, 'I just got married, so I can't come.'
> "The servant came back and reported this to his master.
> Then the owner of the house became angry and ordered
> his servant, 'Go out quickly into the streets and alleys of the
> town and bring in the poor, the crippled, the blind and the
> lame.' "'Sir,' the servant said, 'what you ordered has been
> done, but there is still room.' "Then the master told his ser-
> vant, 'Go out to the roads and country lanes and compel
> them to come in, so that my house will be full. I tell you,
> not one of those who were invited will get a taste of my
> banquet.'" – Luke 14:15-24

The greatest adversary of our love for God are not attacks from
demons, but the blessings themselves which God has given us,
and the deadliest enemies for our appetite for God are the simple pleasures of life. Your work, fixing your house and spending
time with your family (oxen, and fields, and marriage) can keep
you out of the kingdom of heaven if you allow them to occupy
the place in your heart that belongs to God alone. That is why
Jesus said, *"In the same way, those of you who do not give up
everything you have cannot be my disciples"* (Luke 14:33). When
any of these things replaces our appetite for God Himself, it is
very subtle; the idolatry is scarcely recognizable, it is almost un-
detectable, and therefore difficult to correct, unless we humble
ourselves and rely on the revelation of the Holy Spirit.

At this point, I want to be especially emphatic to those of us
reading this book who have a call to ministry, or work in a
ministry. It is important that you realize that just because we
work in a ministry it does not mean that we are dedicated to

God, or that God is first in our lives. Work in a ministry is just that: work. Our relationship with God is something personal and different from just getting things done for the ministry to function correctly. As a matter of fact, our work in the ministry can consume us and take the place that belongs only to God. Do not be fooled and do not give yourself excuses if your personal time and communion with God has dwindled because you are "busy serving God." We need to repent and put the natural things we do for the ministry aside, to seek God first and foremost.

Fasting forces us to test ourselves

"Do I really hunger for God? Do I miss Him? Do I long for Him?" Or, "Am I ok without God? Have I begun to be content with His gifts? Do I no longer miss His presence?" Christian fasting tests what desires control us. Desires for other things are our true enemies. The only weapon that will triumph over these desires is to periodically voluntarily deny ourselves these things in order to obtain a deeper hunger for God.

The reason your hunger for God is so weak is not because God is not good and He cannot satisfy your soul, it is because you have voluntarily chosen to stuff yourself with other things. By fasting, we are seeking to realign our hearts' affections with God and His will, so that we may earnestly love Him and pray for His will to be done and be accomplished on the earth. When we fast things, we are saying to the Lord, "I love you Lord, more than anything in the world, and I want to desire Your will above my own".

On those days we are fasting, we need to be focused on God. Just because we fast and pray does not mean that God is pleased with our sacrifice. If our hearts are not right before Him, any fasting we do will be meaningless and in vain. You should voluntarily fast regularly throughout the year to increase your hunger for God, and to know what is hidden in your heart.

It is time to ask: "Can you eat of God and be satisfied? Can you find spiritual communion with God, not just to be able to cope with life, but to flourish and rejoice in Him over what you are experiencing in your circumstances right now?" The answer is yes!

You will always be tempted to rationalize away your need to fast and pray to seek God. Instead, you will be inclined to indulge yourself in other things. We must resist that temptation because temporal things will never satisfy the desire of our souls. Apostle Paul said, *"Everything is lawful for me, but I will not become the slave of anything or be brought under its power"* (1 Corinthians 6:12 ampc). Fasting reveals the measure of control or degree of influence that television, computers, or whatever else we have submitted ourselves to day after day, have over us, to the point of becoming a priority in our lives over God Himself.

Fasting leads us to desire more of God

The more deeply you walk with Christ, the hungrier you get for Him. The more you want "all the fullness of God," the more you want to be done with sin. The more you desire God, the more you will have God's heart.

If you do not feel a strong passion and desire for God, it is because your soul is stuffed with other things, and there is no room for Him. You are not hungry for Him; therefore, you are continuously giving excuses not to come to the dinner He has prepared for you. God did not create you like that. There is an appetite and a passion for God that He placed in all of us, and it can be awakened! Today I invite you to make a decision to turn from the dangers of putting things before God (as idols) and to say to God with a simple voluntary fast, "this much, O God, I love You and I want You. I long for You and for the manifestation of Your glory in my life!"

We will be able to say as the psalmist said:

> *You, God, are my God, earnestly I seek you; I thirst for you, my whole being longs for you, in a dry and parched land where there is no water. I have seen you in the sanctuary and beheld your power and your glory. Because your love is better than life, my lips will glorify you. I will praise you as long as I live, and in your name, I will lift up my hands. I will be fully satisfied as with the richest of foods; with singing lips my mouth will praise you. – Psalm 63:1-5*

Through the process of fasting correctly, your passion and love for God will grow and flourish.

Chapter 6

How to Receive the Fullness of God Through the Holy Spirit

Without the Holy Spirit, we cannot even begin to draw near to God. We need the Holy Spirit for everything. We cannot believe in God and have true faith in the finished work of Jesus on the cross without the Holy Spirit indwelling our inner man. Why? Because we cannot manufacture faith in our own ability. Faith is supernatural and its origin is God. Without the Spirit of God, we will have a formula or a methodology, but not genuine faith, because faith comes from God. We need God's Holy Spirit to receive God's faith.

The Holy Spirit wants to abide in every area of our inner man, specifically the innermost part of our being, as is stated in

Ephesians 3:16 (AMPC) *"May He grant you out of the rich treasury of His glory to be strengthened and reinforced with mighty power in the inner man by the [Holy] Spirit [Himself indwelling your innermost being and personality]."* This innermost being and personality is our subconscious. This is where there are countless memories and experiences that we acquired throughout the course of our lives, and these things formed our present personality and belief system. In our subconscious, reside traditions, acquired knowledge, opinions of men, bad and good experiences, etc. However, we cannot recall most of those memories because they are hidden in our subconscious. Nevertheless, these hidden things still govern our beliefs and patterns of thought, and drive our behavior every day. They hinder our ability to walk with the faith of God.

Praying mentally, without faith

There are many times we pray superficially, without faith. And there are many times we praise and worship God superficially, without faith, we do it just mentally. As a matter of fact, we always start praying, praising and worshiping God this way; superficially and mentally. However, there has to be a moment where we shift, where we surpass our intellect and reasoning, and our conscious and subconscious thoughts. Reaching that place past our intellect is easier said than done. Why? Because to do this we have to surrender our all to God, and allow His Holy Spirit access and habitat to the deepest level of not only our conscious mind, but also our subconscious mind. He must indwell our innermost being, even our subconscious. This indwelling is not automatic. The Holy Spirit will abide in us only to the level we surrender and yield to Him.

You and I are not fully aware of the thought patterns that were established in our subconscious throughout our lives. However, they are there, and they are continuously influencing our ability to believe in God, limiting our ability to act in faith, and limiting our actions. There are countless things in our subconscious minds that are subtly affecting our conscious mind. These experiences and forgotten memories are restricting us from reaching levels of communion and intimacy we could have with God.

We desperately need the Holy Spirit to enter our subconscious minds and sweep out every opposing thought that continuously rises to argue against the knowledge of God, the love of Christ and the truths of the gospel of His Kingdom. We need these things to be taken out and dealt with forever. We cannot deal with them superficially and expect to live a life of faith. We need to deal with them once and for all. It is like deleting an email from your email list; you have only **partially** dealt with it because it remains in your computer's trash bin, and it is not fully gone until you go in the trash, mark it, and click: "Delete forever!"

Until we say to God, "Father, through Your Holy Spirit I ask You to transform my inner man, change my perception of all things at the level of my subconscious. Indwell my innermost being and personality, my character, nature, my makeup, my disposition, temperament, soul, my mind, conscious and subconscious, and all of my inner being. Erase every thought pattern that opposes You at the level of my subconscious.

Possess me. May I fully experience Your amazing, endless love, and that I may come to know practically, through personal experience and by true faith, the love of Christ."

In a similar way, when we memorize a Bible verse, we are doing it mentally or superficially. This is not the same as having God's Word abide in us, which brings revelation and the wisdom of God. Where the Word and the Spirit of God abide, there is wisdom. When we allow God, through His Holy Spirit, to indwell our innermost being, we have more than mere knowledge, we acquire wisdom and understanding, we have revelation, the spirit of intelligence, the spirit of wisdom, of counsel and power and might and the fear of the Lord. (See Isaiah 11:2). This is very different from merely memorizing a Bible verse with our minds.

John 15:7 says: "If you remain in me and my words remain in you, ask whatever you wish, and it will be done for you." In other words, you will see visible results of your faith. This verse is saying that this profound abiding of Christ and His Word in our innermost being produces true faith, faith that works, that produces a visible testimony. It is not how much you pray that gives visible results to the circumstances, it is how much you believe and exercise true faith when you pray, that brings visible results to your prayers.

Do you want the fullness of God?

If you want the fullness of God, then pray what the apostle Paul prayed.

For this reason, I kneel before the Father, from whom every family in heaven and on earth derives its name. I pray that out of his glorious riches he may strengthen you with power through his Spirit in your inner being, so that Christ may dwell in your hearts through faith. And I pray that you, being rooted and established in love, may have power, together with all the Lord's holy people, to grasp how wide and long and high and deep is the love of Christ, and to know this love that surpasses knowledge—that you may be filled to the measure of all the fullness of God.
– Ephesians 3:14-19

When you pray inviting the Holy Spirit to indwell your innermost being and personality, know that you will be spiritually energized with God's power in your inner man.

We need to be set free and activated in the innermost part of our being by the Holy Spirit to be established in true faith. We need the Holy Spirit to cleanse our subconscious, that part of our soul that is storing traditions, reasoning, faith in men, disappointments, and so forth. We are only as good as our soul is cleansed. (See 3 John 1:2).

How do we detox our soul, mind, conscious and subconscious mind, for the Holy Spirit to be able to plant God's faith?

Pray This Prayer with All Your Heart:

Father God: I repent from and renounce, at the level of my subconscious mind (the innermost part of my character and personality), to every hidden thought or opinion of pride, arrogance, rebellion, iniquity, sin and independence that rises against the knowledge of Christ. I renounce to every thought pattern and stronghold of doubt and un-belief, insecurity and limitation that has been established in my subconscious —not just my conscious— and I ask You Heavenly Father, that through Your Holy Spirit, You penetrate the deepest parts of my soul, which include my sub-conscious. Lord, remove forever every thought pattern and stronghold that is there that has opposed You.

Cleanse my subconscious with the blood of Jesus and take out all the contamination that has influenced me to act contrary to Your will, even subconscious influences affect-ing my actions against You, resisting You. Everything that arises and resists You, all this contamination, all of this corruption, remove it from me, delete it forever, undo it and uproot it by the power of the blood of Jesus and the power of your Holy Spirit, renew my mind and renew my spirit within me.

In its place, Father, deposit Your faith, true faith, Your power, Your grace, Your living Word, and a greater level of Your amazing endless love. Fill me and flood me with who You are. Energize and strengthen my innermost man with Your presence that You may truly dwell in my sub-conscious, and rule and govern my life.

Father God, as I yield to you, grant to me to be energized with power by your Spirit in my innermost man. Plant mustard seed faith now in the fertile ground of my conscious and subconscious, mind and heart, that I may be filled with Your fullness.

Chapter 7

Abiding in Christ Through the Holy Communion

The teachings of Christian doctrine and principles are essential to the body of Christ. (Hebrews 5:12; 6:1-3) However, there is a realm that surpasses instruction which each of us needs to reach, the realm where we learn how to live and walk in the revelation of God's Word. Our walk with Christ depends on how we respond to the Holy Spirit of God when He quickens us to obey and act on what we have heard and learned of God's Word. With this in mind, let's discuss a biblical doctrine, or instruction, that was established by the Lord Jesus Christ, which many Christians are not practicing as they should, and that is the principle of the partaking of the Holy Communion.

The holy communion

The Holy Communion is symbolic of the eternal covenant that we entered through the sacrifice of the body of the Lord Jesus

Christ, which restored our relationship with God the Father, and is the basis of Christianity. This covenant is the new and living way, as per Hebrews 10:19-20 *"Therefore, brothers and sisters, since we have confidence to enter the Most Holy Place by the blood of Jesus, by a new and living way opened for us through the curtain, that is, His body."*

In the upper room, Jesus instructed His disciples on how to take the Holy Communion: *"And he took bread, gave thanks and broke it, and gave it to them, saying, "This is my body given for you; do this in remembrance of me. In the same way, after the supper he took the cup, saying, "This cup is the new covenant in my blood, which is poured out for you.* (Lucas 22:19-20)

When we partake of the Holy Communion, we must keep in mind this is a time to activate the power of redemption over our lives, and a time to express our gratitude for the atonement (reconciliation with God) which was obtained by the death of Jesus on the cross of Calvary.

The mystery of the Holy Communion

The greatest inheritance we have is what Jesus accomplished on the cross of Calvary for us. However, if we do not appropriate the power of the finished work of Christ on the cross, by faith, as we partake of the Holy Communion, its power will not manifest in our lives.

Everything we need was paid for on the cross of Jesus, and it can manifest in our lives through faith. We can access everything

Jesus died to give us, when we receive revelation of the mystery of the Holy Communion and act in faith to experience its power in a living mighty way.

> *They triumphed over him by the blood of the Lamb and by the word of their testimony; they did not love their lives so much as to shrink from death. – Revelation 12:11*

When we take the Holy Communion, we do not have to plead the blood of Jesus, instead we need to partake of it. Taking the Holy Communion is not a matter of pleading for the blood to work on our behalf, because to plead is to ask for something from someone to the point of begging, or supplicating. We do not have to beg or struggle to receive what has already been given to us through Christ. It is already ours by grace through faith. There is a difference between supplication and fellowship, which implies partaking. To partake is to **experience and encounter**, to eat or drink something; to possess, own, hold, engage in and enter into something. We can, and should, appropriate ourselves of and partake in the benefits of the blood and body of Jesus in remembrance of Him and what He paid for at the cross. We can freely enter in, possess, experience and encounter its benefits by faith and those benefits will be made flesh within us. We will have an experience with the power that was released at the cross of Calvary!

> *He who did not spare his own Son, but gave him up for us all-how will he not also, along with him, graciously give us all things? – Romans 8:32*

Throughout church history, God's people have had little manifestations of many of God's blessings in their lives because of their lack of revelation of the mystery of the Holy Communion and how to unleash its power. They have missed out on things like healings, miracles, unity among the brethren, holiness, removal of curses, prosperity and divine protection that could have been obtained through faith by partaking of the body and blood of Jesus through the Holy Communion.

What is in the Blood of Jesus?

God's nature is in the blood of Jesus. When Jesus was conceived in Mary's womb through the Holy Spirit, the Holy Spirit operated as the vehicle, whereas God the Father contributed His nature to unite humanity and His divinity in the body of Christ. Eternity penetrated time and inhabited a physical body for the first time. However, now God continues to become flesh on earth today through Jesus' church that has received revelation of the covenant of the body and blood of Jesus; except now we are not conceived in the natural as Jesus was conceived in Mary's womb, but in the spirit.

What happens when we take the Holy Communion?

- **We dwell in Jesus and He dwells in us**

When we continually take the Holy Communion, we are continually dwelling in Him (Jesus) and as a result, God the Father is dwelling in us. We are proclaiming we are one with Jesus, and therefore, one with God the Father through Jesus Christ. We are abiding, or dwelling in Jesus and He is abiding in us.

When the Word of God says that we dwell or abide in Jesus, it is stating that that is where we live every day.

> *He who feeds on My flesh and drinks My blood dwells continually in Me, and I [in like manner dwell continually] in him. Just as the living Father sent Me and I live by (through, because of) the Father, even so whoever continues to feed on Me [whoever takes Me for his food and is nourished by Me] shall [in his turn] live through and because of Me. – John 6:56-57* AMPC

Through partaking of the Holy Communion, we dwell in Him, we become one with God the Father, the Creator of the universe. Heaven and earth are united in this act. Humanity is united to God's divine nature again, and transformed into His image. Through the partaking of the Holy Communion, eternity penetrates time and inhabits our physical bodies here on earth as we become one with God!

The son of God became flesh when He was divinely begotten by the Holy Spirit, and today He continues to become flesh in His church through the Holy Spirit when we partake of the Holy Communion with revelation and when we become one with Him through eating His flesh and drinking His blood.

John 6:55-56 states: *"For my flesh is real food and my blood is real drink. Whoever eats my flesh and drinks my blood remains in me, and I in them."* Jesus, who is the living Word, is true food and drink; a form of food that quickens our spirit. We can have Jesus present, manifesting and abiding in us every day, because eating is something we do daily. We can be quickened with eternal life every day because of the sacrifice of Jesus. When we eat His flesh, and drink His blood we remain in Him. To remain indicates that we are continuously there, we are continuously filled, and continuously have communion with the Lord.

Your communion with Jesus cannot be an occasional event. It must be a continual communion with Him, in the same manner He is continually united with the Father. In order to receive life, you must receive Jesus, the bread of life, on a continuous basis. Just as the physical body is not sustained by eating just once, or only once in a while, neither can our spirit be sustained by eating of Jesus only every now and then.

> *Then Jesus declared, "I am the bread of life. Whoever comes to me will never go hungry, and whoever believes in me will never be thirsty." – John 6:35*

Unfortunately, because of lack of revelation and lack of appropriation of the Holy Communion, there are a lot of Christians walking around spiritually weak, disconnected from the source of life; hungry and thirsty.

- **We receive God's type of life**

When we take the Holy Communion, we receive God's nature, His type of life, which is eternal life. Eternal life is not just life without end, it is God's nature, His power, His glory, His authority, His strength, His love, all that He is. All of who He is becomes one with us. Jesus said: *"I am the living bread that came down from heaven. Whoever eats this bread will live forever. This bread is my flesh, which I will give for the life of the world." Then the Jews began to argue sharply among themselves, "How can this man give us his flesh to eat?" Jesus said to them, "Very truly I tell you, unless you eat the flesh of the Son of Man and drink his blood, you have no life in you. Whoever eats my flesh and drinks my blood has eternal life, and I will raise them up at the last day"* (John 6:51-54).

Also, through Jesus' flesh and His blood (as we take the Holy Communion) God's presence and power manifests in our lives. We receive His supernatural power; spiritual strength and ability, we are made able and sustained by Him.

- **We become one with the Father**

When we become one with Jesus through the Holy Communion, anything we ask in His name, we will receive it, because Jesus is one with the Father. He said we would do greater things than the works that He did if we believe that He is one with the Father: Miracles and great works are evidence of unity with God the Father.

Don't you believe that I am in the Father, and that the Father is in me? The words I say to you I do not speak on my own authority. Rather, it is the Father, living in me, who is doing his work. Believe me when I say that I am in the Father and the Father is in me; or at least believe on the evidence of the works themselves. Very truly I tell you, whoever believes in me will do the works I have been doing, and they will do even greater things than these, because I am going to the Father. And I will do whatever you ask in my name, so that the Father may be glorified in the Son. You may ask me for anything in my name, and I will do it. – John 14:10-14

A lot of God's people today are weak and have no power because they have not approached the Holy Communion with revelation and genuine faith. We have been ignorant of its impact in the spiritual and the natural world. By our approaching the Holy Communion as a ritual, or a religious act, and partaking of it strictly as a formality, it has virtually no effect on us; the church has lost the essence of what the Holy Communion truly is, and, consequently, what it can do.

- **We receive His resurrection life**

    For if we have been united with him in a death like his, we will certainly also be united with him in a resurrection like his. – Romans 6:5

When we confessed Jesus as Lord and Savior and that God raised Him from the dead, we were born again, and each time we take the Holy Communion —in remembrance of His death and resurrection— we become one with Him and with His death, but more importantly with His resurrection and life. This is such a great mystery, incomprehensible to the human mind, there are no words to express our gratitude towards God for what He has accomplished through the death and resurrection of His son, Jesus Christ, on our behalf.

- **Times of refreshing and restitution will come**

If we take the Holy Communion with faith, times of refreshing and restitution will be activated so that everything is restored to us. Seeking God and true repentance will cause the refreshing and restitution times to be put into motion in our lives, so that everything that was distorted by sin while we were separated from God is restored.

> *Repent, then, and turn to God, so that your sins may be wiped out, that times of refreshing may come from the Lord, and that he may send the Messiah, who has been appointed for you—even Jesus. Heaven must receive him until the time comes for God to restore everything, as he promised long ago through his holy prophets. – Acts. 3:19-21*

This restitution will affect our health, our broken hearts, our finances, our broken relationships. Through this restitution, we are delivered from every type of curse and every type of disease. All aspects of God's will are restored to our lives. Jesus' flesh and blood are the antidote to all types of curses, sickness, disease, etc., none can remain, that is, if we partake of the Holy Communion with revelation.

- **The Holy Communion brings love and unity among brethren**

We receive God's type of love to be able to walk in true love and fellowship with others. In the book of Acts, we can see the fellowship, or the common life, that was shared by the early

Christian believers in Jerusalem and why they were capable of having true fellowship:

> *And they steadfastly persevered, devoting themselves constantly to the instruction and fellowship of the apostles, **to the breaking of bread [including the Lord's Supper]** and prayers. And a sense of awe (reverential fear) came upon every soul, and many wonders and signs were performed through the apostles (the special messengers). And all who believed (who adhered to and trusted in and relied on Jesus Christ) were united and [together] they had everything in common; And they sold their possessions (both their landed property and their movable goods) and distributed the price among all, according as any had need. And day after day they regularly assembled in the temple with united purpose, and in their homes they broke bread [including the Lord's Supper]. They partook of their food with gladness and simplicity and generous hearts, constantly praising God and being in favor and goodwill with all the people; and the Lord kept adding [to their number] daily those who were being saved [from spiritual death].*
> *– Acts 2: 42-47*

It was in the breaking of the bread, called communion, that the apostles recognized, celebrated, and received the riches in Christ Jesus through His death and resurrection. Communion is associated with various spiritual purposes, one of which is bringing love and unity among brethren. When they joined in the Lord's Supper, they were uniting with other believers who were also in Christ. By their joint participation in Christ, they were made one in Him, in obedience to Jesus' instructions: "And he took bread, gave thanks and broke it, and gave it to them, saying, "This is my body given for you; do this in remembrance of me" (Luke 22:19). Jesus' final prayer to the Father was that we would be made one as He and the Father are one.

> *I pray that they will all be one, just as you and I are one—as you are in me, Father, and I am in you. And may they be in us so that the world will believe you sent me.*
> *– John 17:21* NLT

Only the Holy Spirit, through Jesus' sacrifice can accomplish this unity as we partake of the Holy Communion with revelation that we are made one in Christ through it.

• **We receive the fear of God that leads us to holiness**

We should approach God and the Holy Communion with awe, reverence, fear and trembling, recognizing who God is, and what He has freely and graciously given us through His son Jesus Christ. When we partake of the Holy Communion with revelation, we receive the fear of God which leads us to holiness.

Most Christians are ignorant of the powerful benefits of taking the Holy Communion as one of the Biblical principles to a successful Christian life, and therefore, they hardly ever partake of it. When they do take the Holy Communion, they do so without revelation, faith or reverence and consequently, there are no evident effects of its benefits. The result of this is that the body of Christ on earth, for the most part, is sick, indebted, weak, powerless, divided, it lacks genuine love and is filled with gossip, contention and division. This is the complete opposite of what God designed the body of Christ to do and to be.

It is time to take the Holy Communion seriously and regularly eat Jesus' flesh and drink His blood as He commanded us to do so, as not to be weak, sick or even die prematurely. We do not have to be sick and infirmed if we discern with faith and appreciation the body of Jesus Christ, the son of God.

> *In the same way, after supper he took the cup, saying, "This cup is the new covenant in my blood; do this, whenever you drink it, in remembrance of me." For whenever you eat this bread and drink this cup, you proclaim the Lord's death until he comes. So then, whoever eats the bread or drinks the cup of the Lord in an unworthy manner will be guilty of sinning against the body and blood of the Lord. Everyone ought to examine themselves before they eat of the bread and drink from the cup. For those who eat and drink without discerning the body of Christ eat and drink judgment on themselves. That is why many among you are weak and sick, and a number of you have fallen asleep. But if we were more discerning with regard to ourselves, we would not come under such judgment.*
> *– 1 Corinthians 11:25-31*

Take the Holy Communion now

I invite you, dear reader, if you are able to do so, to take the Holy

Communion right now. If now is not convenient, take it during your next personal devotional time. You do not have to wait to go to church to take the Holy Communion. Simply pour a small amount of juice in a cup and break off a piece of bread. The juice does not have to be grape juice, it can be any juice.

Pray and confess any known sins before God, then as you eat the bread, declare that you are eating the flesh of Jesus and, therefore, receiving its benefits. Example: I am being set free from all curses, sickness and poverty. The flesh of Jesus and His blood are the antidotes to curses. Curses are not only incantations invoked by witches or warlocks, they can come in the form of words spoken by other people against us in gossip and hatred, remember that the power of life and death is in the tongue, so people either speak words of life or words of death. There are also generational curses from sins of our ancestors, or our own past sins causing a type of death in some area of our lives.

Eat the bread slowly, and as you eat, declare that you are receiving God's divine nature, more of His eternal life, His supernatural power, His love. Thank Him for coming to live within you. Pray and declare according to how the Holy Spirit leads you. If you are ill or have a terminal disease, declare you are set free from its deadly influence over your body by the power that Jesus released at the cross when He died in your place. He broke the power of sickness and disease, and even the spirit of death itself. Drink the juice and declare you drink the blood of Jesus that cleanses you from all unrighteousness and sets you free from all oppression, emotional or mental oppression, or depression. Declare restoration to every area of your life, spirit, soul and body; also, declare restoration over your finances, over broken relationships, and declare salvation for your household, and any other declaration you discern needs to be made. As you take the Holy Communion in faith, and with revelation of the source of its power, know that you are being transformed into the image of Christ, as you act in faith and in obedience to God's Word.

Supernatural power is released as you take the Holy Communion

Do this as often as you can; whether it be every day, every other day, twice a week, or once a week. It is a source from the life of God through Christ Jesus. Do not take the Holy Communion with a religious mindset. Know that the elements themselves, the bread and the juice, have no power in and of themselves: the supernatural power that is released comes from the flesh and blood of Jesus that was sacrificed on our behalf, and that power is released in the spiritual dimension and impacts the natural dimension every time we make remembrance of it. It is released according to your faith and obedience to Jesus' instructions, and then it manifests in the natural realm in many different ways, according to our need and our faith. You will see a result of this action of faith in your life in many areas as you continue to partake of the Holy Communion in the right way, with the right mindset, with revealed knowledge of the power behind this mandate Jesus required us to do.

Even if you are not able to comprehend with your mind the mysteries of the Holy Communion and the mandate to eat His body and drink His blood, you can by-pass your reasoning and act in faith, and you will see the results of obedience and faith every time. As you do it regularly, you will feel the mighty presence of God setting you free every time, and increasingly, you will have manifestations of deliverance (such as coughing, crying, etc.) Most of the time we are not aware of what we are being delivered from because the Holy Spirit does not reveal it to us, however, there are times He does. In my case, when I have taken the Holy Communion, I know that many times I am being set free from condemning words spoken by others in judgment and criticism. I literally feel the power of God setting my body free. We need to regularly take the Holy Communion and make faith filled declarations over our health, family, relationships, and finances.

And when he had given thanks, he broke it and said, "This is my body, which is for you; do this in remembrance of me." – 1 Corinthians 11:24

But the Comforter, which is the Holy Ghost, whom the Father will send in My name, He shall teach you all things, and bring all things to your remembrance, whatsoever I have said unto you. – John 14:26 KJV

We can declare the power of life in the blood of Jesus with our mouths because life is in the blood. When the power of the blood is declared, the covenant we have with God manifests. Every time you declare the blood of Jesus, a portal is opened in heaven. Therefore, in like manner, every time you take the Holy Communion, a portal opens in heaven, demonic activity stops, and angels are released to protect you.

Prayer to take the Holy Communion

I invite you, dear reader, to declare the following prayer out loud as you take the Holy Communion today:

> *Father God, I activate the power of the covenant of the blood and the body of Christ Jesus through the Holy Communion as I make remembrance of what Jesus died to give me. I bypass my reason and I act in faith today, knowing I will see the results of my obedience of taking the Holy Communion with revelation of its power. Today, by faith, I eat and drink Jesus' body and blood and I experience and encounter the benefits of His sacrifice on the cross. I receive the fear of God as I take the Holy Communion with reverence and trembling, recognizing that You are God.*

> *I repent from all my sins. As I drink the juice, I am drinking the blood of Jesus which cleanses me from all unrighteousness. Thank You for its delivering power. I am being set free right now from demonic oppression, from all types of curses, from words that have condemned me, from judgment and criticism. I declare the power of the blood of Jesus with my mouth and the covenant that I have with God. As I do this, a portal opens in heaven and demonic activity stops, and the angels of God are released to protect my family and myself. Your blood and Your flesh, Jesus, are an antidote to all types of curses, sickness and disease, and I receive that antidote today.*

As I take the Holy Communion with faith, *times of refreshing shall come to my life, and times of restitutions of all the things that were lost or distorted by sin. Father God, you refresh my soul. This restitution touches my health, my broken heart, any broken relationships and sets me free from emotional and mental oppression. I declare restoration in every area of my life, my spirit, my soul and my body, by the power of God. I declare that through partaking of the Holy Communion I am continuously dwelling in Jesus and He is continuously dwelling in me, and I become one with you God the Father, through Jesus Christ. I will never be hungry or thirsty again, because Jesus is the bread of life and He said that whoever comes to Him will never go hungry and will never be thirsty.*

Father God, *I receive and activate your eternal life in me, Your type of life, Your nature, Your power, glory and authority, Your strength, Your love and all that You are. As I take the Holy Communion I receive resurrection life and resurrection power, because I am partaking and becoming one with Christ. Romans 6:5 says that if we have become one with Christ in His death, we will be one with Him in being raised from the dead to new life. Therefore, I receive Jesus' resurrection power today. As I take the Holy Communion, I also receive Your supernatural love to be able to walk in true love and fellowship with others. I become one with my brothers and sisters in Christ, just as Jesus is one with You Father, we also become one in You. As I take the Holy Communion today, I am being transformed into the image of Christ.*

Thank You for the power that is being released right now in the spiritual dimension which is impacting the natural dimension! I take advantage to the fullest of what Jesus conquered at the cross, in order to live in complete health by God's supernatural power. By taking the Holy Communion in obedience to Jesus' command to eat His flesh and drink His blood, I possess my inheritance to Kingdom health. At the cross by Jesus' wounds, divine health burst violently into existence for all to partake of it, just as eternal life for all was supplied. I appropriate healing power from Jesus' wounds for my body as I eat the bread symbolizing His body. The Lord is my Healer and His wounds still heal today! I live by the power that was activated at the cross. I receive health, strength and vitality in my physical body because of the unity of my spirit with Jesus. As we become one in the spirit, my body becomes one with divine health, and sickness cannot prevail. The power manifested at the Cross of Jesus is the only thing I need to live in health and to prosper.

I command divine relationships that God has preordained for me and for my family to come into fruition and be fulfilled for the mutual benefit of each, and for the glory of God. These relationships are set free and must manifest now by the power of the cross of Jesus as I take the Holy Communion. I prophesy to those who must join me or my family, to supernaturally come and find me now. I declare those that will be a blessing to my life and to my family, according to God's purposes on earth, to come into *communion and unity with me. I declare in the name of Jesus, and by His great power, that those who I am supposed to be a blessing to, also come into my life. All barriers of distance, demonic opposition or delay withholding these relationships is broken by the power that was manifested at the cross of Jesus, as I take the Holy Communion today and eat Jesus' flesh and drink His blood. I declare people are added unto me that will be faithful and remain faithful. I call them at this time. Come now! I declare that the blood of Jesus that runs in them and runs in me binds us into perfect unity for the glory of God. Heavenly Father, You do this by Your great power.*

I will no longer struggle financially, *I will no longer have to work in painful labor clawing at the earth to make it yield fruit for me to prosper. Instead, I receive divine provision and prosperity, and I know that as God the Father has given me His dear son, He will also freely give me together with Him, all things! I declare that the financial instruments that the Father has already preordained for me and my family since before the foundation of the world, enter into contact with us and come into our lives at this time and as God has abundantly preordained. At the cross, through grace, Jesus became poor so that through His poverty, I might become rich.*

Thank You, *my God and my King, for the power of the finished work of Jesus on the cross!*

Dear reader, your walk with Christ consists of the response you give to the Holy Spirit of God when He quickens you to obey and act on what you have heard and learned of His Word. Therefore, put into practice, on a regular basis from now on, the revelation of the Holy Communion you have just received, and you will surely experience the manifestation of the risen Christ in your life.

Chapter 8

A Word for Weary Christians

A s I am writing this book, I know in my spirit that there will be many good Christian women reading it; women that because of stress have become so spiritually dry that they have said to themselves, "I cannot live another day like this, feeling overwhelmed and disconnected from God. I have lost my passion to be in His presence." If this is your condition, it is imperative that today you identify and renounce to the stress that has hindered your relationship with God and held you back from encountering Him on a personal level!

Are you weary and stressed?

Stress is a barrier that alienates people from God. Countless Christians start as passionate believers, but stress, daily responsibilities and busy lifestyles rob them of the opportunity to live in communion with God. Since we cannot enter God's presence when we are overwhelmed and stressed, consequently, we may be slowly drying out spiritually, becoming wearier and overburdened every day that passes. Are you slowly becoming a weary and stressed believer?

When we speak of stress, we are not only talking about the normal responsibilities of daily life; we are also talking about excessive pressures that demonic spirits of anxiety and fear instigate to oppress people and keep them in bondage. This type of stress consumes a person physically, mentally, emotionally and even spiritually.

The climax of stress is depression.

When a demonic spirit has been at work long enough, stress reaches the state of depression. Depression drives people into a self-destructive mode. A depressed person is one who loses all hope, because they see no end to their affliction. Those under this type of stress, find themselves on an endless treadmill going around in circles, thinking that if they can just get everything under control, they will be all right. However, that culmination is never attained and the vicious cycle continues and escalates.

Stress puts the burden on the person to perform, and the result is that when they are stressed, they start to depend on their own abilities and strengths (which are at best very limited), instead of relying on the omnipotence of God and His power. The impossible situations that we all face in life can only be overcome with the supernatural power of God. When we try to overcome them ourselves, we become weary.

Jesus' solution for weary christians

Jesus says: *"Come to Me, all you who are weary and burdened, and I will give you rest."* (Matthew 11:28). This place of rest is where I want to take you as you read this book; to a place where you can receive freedom for your soul and renew your fellowship with God.

The first thing we must do is come to Jesus and repent for allowing stress to oppress us; it is a command from God that we not be anxious about anything, Philippians 4:6-7 says: *"Do not be anxious about anything, but in every situation, by prayer and petition, with thanksgiving, present your requests to God. And the peace of God, which transcends all understanding, will guard your hearts and your minds in Christ Jesus."*

Prayer to renounce stress

Dear reader, I invite you to pray now the following prayer:

Father God, I repent for allowing stress, oppression, worry and anxiety to take control of my mind, my heart and my soul. I renounce to undue burden, oppression, worry and stress. I make the decision to depend upon You instead of carrying the heavy burden of depending on my strength. I renounce to the temptation of trying to do in my own abilities, those things which can only be accomplished by Your supernatural power.

I renounce to every yoke of bondage that stress has put upon me. I close the door to the demonic oppression of anxiety and brokenness of spirit, and I renounce to the spirit of depression. I put aside every burden that has entangled me and weighed me down.

I renounce to all emotional and physical stress. I renounce to all anxiety and fear of the future. I renounce to affliction in my soul that causes undue burden, brokenness of spirit and fear. I renounce every demonic oppression that wants to make me good-for-nothing! I close the doors of my heart and mind to brokenness, and I declare that what is bound in heaven I can bind here on earth, and the oppression of stress that has tried to engulf my spirit is bound on earth as it is bound in heaven.

I surrender each impossibility to You Lord, I give You that yoke, and instead I receive the yoke of Your unfailing grace that empowers me to do what I cannot do in my own strength.

I renounce to the effects of stress that want to kill me prematurely. I renounce to stress and its related illnesses, and declare they leave my body in Jesus' name: I renounce the spirit of infirmity attached to stress that causes all types of diseases including cancer, diabetes, high blood pressure, blurred vision, migraines, arthritis pain and all other related illnesses; I declare that the oppression caused by the spirit of infirmity that had a legal right to inflict my body due to stress, is removed from my life in the name of Jesus! Premature death cannot attack my body, in the name of Jesus!

I renounce to self-imposed burdens and stress that are too heavy for me to carry. I deliver myself from undue burdens and stress imposed by others upon me, that I am not supposed to carry. I deliver myself from mental burdens of fear and anxiety in the name of Jesus. Whatever point of entry that was used by Satan for these burdens to come in through, those entry points are closed now in the name of Jesus, and every oppression leaves now. Stress imposed externally or internally, comes out. I am released from it. Stress imposed by demonic oppression, comes out. Stress imposed by society and the system of this world, leaves me now. All these entry points are closed in the name of Jesus and I am set free! Lord, I receive Your peace that surpasses all understanding. I rest in You, my God. I replace stress, anxiety and a broken spirit, with Your faith, hope and love. I declare the joy of the Lord is my strength and I receive Your healing power now. I am blessed with good health!

Allow me to pray for You dear reader:

Please allow me to pray for you and come into agreement with the previous prayer you have just declared:

Heavenly Father, I rebuke the spirit of stress in Your people, that have renounced to its hold on them, and have commanded it to stop its activity in their lives, in the name of Jesus. I declare that all oppressions of stress, anxiety, fear, worry and undue burdens come out of those who have renounced to it, in the name of Jesus. I declare these demonic spirits are no longer able to overburden Your people, and that they are set free from the spiritual captivity they were placed in by these oppressions, where they walked spiritually dry.

Father*, I put a demand on the delivering power of the finished work of Jesus Christ on the cross and declare that the effects of stress that have wanted to take the lives of Your people prematurely, are broken now. Instead, oh Lord, You give them good health and a long life. Stress and all its related illnesses are bound and cast out and leave their bodies now, in Jesus' name: spirit of infirmity causing all types of diseases related with stress, including cancer, diabetes, high blood pressure, blurred vision, migraines, arthritis pain and all other related illnesses, come out in the name of Jesus! Premature death, come out in the name of Jesus!*

Now Lord*, I ask You to encounter Your people with your peace that surpasses all understanding and heal the broken-hearted. Holy Spirit, come in and heal the broken emotions. Heal everything that was damaged by stress, including their relationship with You Lord; may it be vibrant, may it be full of joy, may it be spontaneous, may it be full of life, may it be a channel of the abundant life Jesus died to give us.*

I declare *that each reader that has renounced to the oppression of stress receives vigor, life, peace and strength, right now, in their inner man, through Your Holy Spirit. I declare per John 7:38 that from within them flow rivers of living water. Thank You, Lord Jesus. Amen!*

To succeed in giving ourselves to God as much as He desires, we must constantly guard our soul from being overly anxious and full of stress, because stress alienates us from the presence of God. Since God is in control and can rectify any situation in a moment, we should not allow ourselves to become greatly concerned with any problem we face. Simply pray about it and practice surrendering yourself to Christ during any difficult circumstances you may face.

If you are troubled by something, know that God is present; walk in faith and trust in Him. Being overly consumed and constantly thinking about problems will burden your soul, because evil begins from within our thoughts. Therefore, the best thing you can do is have a conversation with God wherein you surrender to Him anything that is troubling you and leave it in His hands. Today you can get rid of the restraint of stress, anxiety, and a broken spirit, that have robbed you of a close relationship with God.

You can also conquer the natural aspect of stress

In addition to the spiritual aspect, there is also a natural aspect of stress and anxiety that we must attend to and be able to overcome on a daily basis. We cannot continue to open doors for the demonic spirit of stress to have a legal right to subdue us. The objective is to be set free and stay free. We must also deal with stress in the natural realm daily, in order to close the door to any future demonic oppression. We must learn how to keep all doors closed in our lives, so that this oppressive spirit cannot have a legal entry through which it can return. To make sure all entry points are closed, we must appropriate a very special gift God has already given us. That gift is: To be satisfied and enjoy the life God has given you in spite of the circumstances (be anxious for nothing.) We are told in God's word to take time to enjoy the gifts and life God has given us. It states, *"That each of them may eat and drink, and find satisfaction in all their toil–this is the gift of God"* (Ecclesiastes 3:13).

Practical nuggets of wisdom to defeat stress

How can we appropriate ourselves of the gifts given to us by God, wherein we can be satisfied in all our toils, when we have so many responsibilities, demands on our time and deadlines? Here are some practical nuggets of wisdom for you to act upon. Do these three things and you will be closing the entry points to future oppressions of stress:

- Categorize;
- Prioritize and
- Organize

As you categorize your activities, you will be able to determine which should be given priority. Do those first. Example: Prayer and communion with God is a priority. Then separate time for the many other different things you do on a regular basis. The Word says, *"There is a time for everything, and a season for every activity under the heavens"* (Ecclesiastes 3:1). There is a time to do every type of activity. Therefore, you need to set aside time to do them and try to stick to the times you set. However, do not be too rigid with your schedule; know that you will need to be flexible at times.

Some valuable advice to accomplish this is:

- *Go to bed early* so you can get up earlier. Wake up earlier every day to pray, and to prepare ahead for your day.
- *Learn to rest*, set times for it. There will be times in your life that the most spiritual thing you can do is rest, because it is essential to your well-being. God Himself rested. Do not use the time you have set aside to rest to do other things. When you are overly tired, you are vulnerable to demonic attacks.
- *Do not allow anxiety* to remain in your life. Give all your anxiety to God in prayer, the moment it presents itself. Learn to take deep breaths, and as you do, instead of becoming anxious, thank God for His blessings. Your spirit will find rest as you release all anxiety to the Lord the moment it comes.
- *Ask God for His grace continuously,* and depend on it. God's grace enables us to do what we cannot do in our own strength.
- *Get help!* One person is too small to do great things. Be creative on how to get the help you need. Learn to delegate. Train others to do what you do.
- *Be creative* about how to get things done in a more efficient or easier way, so the things you must accomplish do not take as much time as they do now, or steal time away from other things God has asked you to do. If you ask your heavenly Father, He will give you His creative ideas.
- *Do not over-commit* to things that will rob you of precious

time to do more important things. If you decide to do something extra for your family or someone dear to you, or to work longer hours, or serve more at church, know it is a sacrifice for a short time that may tire you, but that tiredness will pass and you can recuperate slowly later. Also, be wiser next time about committing to do too many extra things. Do not take all the responsibility upon yourself, and know that at times you will have to say, "no." Learn from your errors, remember the stress you went through during those times in the past when you over-committed, and if you notice you have the habit of over-committing, repent and change.

Do not allow stress to kill your passion

Remember, stress kills passion. The Bible says that if we do not have love and passion for seeking God and His kingdom, we will be nothing, only a resounding gong, and we will gain nothing. (See: 1 Corinthians 13:1-3)

Stress contaminates everything we do to serve God. When stress contaminates our souls, instead of being pure vessels through which the power of God and His love towards others can flow through, we will lack the correct motive to do the things we do, and will become ineffective in everything we commence. To live by faith and please God, we cannot allow stress in our lives. (See Galatians 5:6).

Start making some necessary changes today. After renouncing to stress, remember to categorize, prioritize, and organize.

Do not allow the system of this world to run you ragged, fill you with stress and make you weary, and as a result, cause you to lose the joy of your salvation and your passion for being in the presence of God.

Chapter 9

Bearing Fruit Supernaturally

In the natural world, fruit is the result of a healthy plant producing what it was designed to produce. In the Bible, the word fruit is used to describe a believer's outward actions that are a result of their relationship with God and the condition of their heart. By grace, we have been brought into communion with the Lord, and because of this communion; the Lord likens us to trees that He planted for His own glory (see Isaiah 61:13); trees that will bear abundant fruit for His Kingdom. Throughout God's word, it is evident that the purpose of our constant fellowship with the Lord is that we become fruitful Christians. We are to be women of full growth, mighty in influence, full of God's power, giving abundant fruit every day of our lives, even if in the natural it is difficult or even impossible to be productive.

Some time ago in my time of prayer, I found myself saying, "Lord I do not want to grow beyond my capabilities. I do not want to be overwhelmed." Immediately when I said this, the Holy Spirit was grieved inside of me and I knew that what I had just said was not aligned with God's mindset. My mindset was limiting God's potential from manifesting in me, and I felt the Holy Spirit's conviction. From this experience, the Lord showed me a powerful truth using the parable of the fig tree found in the book of Mark.

On a morning journey to Jerusalem, Jesus and His disciples were coming from Bethany. When Jesus saw a fig tree with leaves on it, He walked to it to see if it had any figs, because He was hungry. When He found none, –not surprisingly, because it wasn't the season for figs–, He declared that no man would ever eat figs from that tree again: *"Seeing in the distance a fig tree in leaf, He went to find out if it had any fruit. When He reached it, He found nothing but leaves, **because it was not the season for figs**. Then he said to the tree, 'May no one ever eat fruit from you again'. And his disciples heard him say it."* (Mark 11:13-14). That evening, as they were returning to Bethany, His disciples noticed that the tree that Jesus cursed had withered. When they asked Him about it, Jesus responded by stating that by faith they could do anything. He told them that if they had faith they could say to a mountain, "Be removed and cast into the sea," and it would happen.

There are several puzzling aspects to this fig tree story. First, why did Jesus, who knew the nature of growing things, and often used that knowledge as a tool for teaching truth, expect to find fruit on the fig tree when it was out of season? Second, why did the tree deserve to be cursed for not having fruit at a time when, by nature, it should not have had any fruit? Sounds unfair, doesn't it? At first sight, the cursing of the fig tree seems to be an outburst of irrational bad temper, for it was not yet the time for the tree to produce figs. However, was it truly an irrational demand on Jesus' part? No, it was not, instead it is a lesson to us that God expects us to perform the impossible. In God's eyes, since our communion is with Him and we are trees planted in His kingdom, we must bear fruit in and out of season, because He has equipped us to do the impossible.

Say the following statement out loud: "God expects me to do the impossible!"

> *He replied… "Truly I tell you, if you have faith as small as a mustard seed, you can say to this mountain, 'Move from here to there,' and it will move. **Nothing will be impossible for you**." – Matthew 17:20*

If you are not doing the impossible you are not pleasing God. "And without faith it is impossible to please God…" (Hebrews 11:6). You may ask, "but Lord, how could I be expected to do what is against my nature? None of the 'other fig trees' are bearing fruit in this season". To which Jesus would reply, "if you have faith as small as a mustard seed…" you will say, "'let there be fruit,' and it will appear".

Jesus used the fig tree as an object lesson of the power of faith to do the impossible, which in this case was to always bear fruit. In God's eyes, there is no excuse for not bearing fruit as believers. We are to use the resources available where we are planted, to achieve the impossible. Because of our fellowship with God, we can become powerful women of God.

Bearing fruit is the direct result of being attached to a favorable environment.

> *The righteous shall flourish like a palm tree, He shall grow like a cedar in Lebanon.* ***Those who are planted in the house of the Lord shall flourish in the courts of our God. They shall still bear fruit in old age;*** *They shall be fresh and flourishing, to declare that the Lord is upright; He is my rock, and there is no unrighteousness in Him.*
> *– Psalm 92:12-15*

The word flourish in the previous verse means to grow or develop in a vigorous way, especially as the result of being planted in a particularly favorable environment. Everything depends upon the environment or soil in which a tree is planted; in our case, it depends upon our abiding in the Lord Jesus, and deriving all our resources from Him. Flourish means to grow, thrive, prosper, do well, increase, bloom, multiply, spring up, blossom, and bear fruit. The verse stated above says the only way we will flourish is by being planted in the house of the Lord.

For a tree branch, it is imperative that it be attached to the tree trunk to be fruitful. Its fertility is a direct result of being attached to a favorable environment, the trunk. Likewise, if a believer abides in Christ, they will bring forth much fruit. (See John 15:7).

Once planted by the Lord, we are to take root downward, and

bring forth fruit upward to His glory. You and I need to grow according to God's glory, not according to our abilities; and that is why God expects us to bear fruit in and out of season. By faith you can declare: "Let there be abundant fruit as I draw from the infinite resources I am planted in!"

As I reread the passage of the fig tree with this revelation, my mindset changed, and I declared that I relinquished and surrendered, and would allow myself to grow beyond my capability. I agreed with God and disagreed with my own reasoning, my limitations and natural impossibilities.

Greater faith can accomplish what Jesus is asking us to do.

Jesus' explanation to the disciples of why he cursed the fig tree (See Matthew 17:20), was based on the revelation that greater faith could have accomplished what He sought to have. It is going to take greater faith than the one you exerted last year, or the faith you are operating in right now, to live victoriously *season after season*, and to be able to bear fruit supernaturally for the glory of God, *year after year*.

We are all, in a sense, fig trees trying to bear fruit acceptable to God in a hostile, almost impossible, environment. As daughters of God, we are expected to be fruitful, even in impossible situations. Why? Because greater faith can accomplish what Jesus is asking of us. Jesus' promise is that if we have faith even as small as a mustard seed, we can do those things that by natural means alone are impossible; we can manifest God's glory!

The book of Romans says, *"And that He might make known the riches of His glory on the vessels of mercy, which He had prepared beforehand for glory"* (Romans 9:23 NKJV)

When God confronted me with this revelation, I told Him, "Lord, I release myself to grow and expand, and will not withhold increasing and bearing fruit for Your glory any longer, due to my personal limitations. I will not make excuses, no matter how legitimate they may seem. I allow Your resources, where I am planted, to bring out supernatural fruit and accelerate growth in me by leaps and bounds. I relinquish and surrender to grow beyond what I can handle, in order to manifest Your glory."

Since the day that I turned over to God my resistance to grow beyond my capabilities in order to manifest His glory, I have seen His glory manifest increasingly in my life. I experienced a recent testimony of this at a Deliverance workshop that I was assigned to minister at my church, King Jesus Ministry, during one of its Schools of the Supernatural Ministry. As I prepared for this class, I inquired of God what specific conditions were affecting His people that would attend the next day. I heard the Lord tell me various things that were very specific, and that, honestly, seemed to me to be very odd. Nevertheless, I wrote them down and the next day, at a point in the ministering I started to declare that the glory of God was present to heal and minister to each person with these conditions. The conditions were:

- A person with a scar on their leg, –caused by abuse from a relative when they were a child–, would be there, and the Lord would set them free from great rejection.

- People who had suffered temporary insanity, loss of their minds, were also going to be set free.
- A person who suffered great rejection because of a cleft palate in the roof of their mouth was going to be healed emotionally and physically.
- Someone with deformed feet was going to be healed physically, and delivered from a spirit of rejection.

The day of the workshop, each one of these conditions was present, and each person that had been mentioned, God ministered to, and was healed and restored! The place exploded with spontaneous supernatural deliverance, people started to scream as they were being set free without anyone touching them.

What I like about impossibilities is that they are a God thing, in other words, they require God to show up. We are connected to an infinitely rich source that is full of provision, which we can access, and from which we can withdraw every type of resource. Nothing is impossible for our God and therefore nothing is impossible for us.

**Dear reader, I invite you to make
the following prayer and declaration out loud:**

Father, I recognize that if I just do the natural and the normal, You will not receive any glory from my life. You receive glory when I do the impossible by faith, when I do what is unexpected and unlikely, when I produce fruit for Your Kingdom, even when all the odds are against me. Therefore Father, I renounce right now to every thought limiting me, telling me that the season of bearing fruit for Your Kingdom has passed in my life. I renounce to those thoughts, I renounce to those words, I renounce to those curses. Father, there is fruit for You in my life at all times because You are the source of my provision, of my substance; and therefore, I can do what is not natural and normal, I can do the unusual and unexpected. I can do the supernatural; what is beyond my capabilities, what I cannot do in my own strength, what is out of the normal range of probability. Thank you Lord Jesus for allowing me to be united with You in such a way and with such intensity, that your power is continuously grafted into me. I am connected to you and as a result I am connected to Your supernatural power. I am able to receive from your infinite resources as the branch receives from the vine. Since I am grounded in love, planted in Your Kingdom, established by Your word and in communion with Your Holy Spirit, nothing is impossible for me.

Father God, I surrender to your will, and I now make the decision to stop withholding Your supernatural accelerated growth and fruitfulness that, to me, may seem out of proportion, out of control, or out of a natural course of growth. I surrender to Your above and beyond. There is no such thing as 'too big' for You, therefore there is no such thing as 'too big' for me. I rely on Your glory. I depend on Your strength and Your provision. I am ready to grow by leaps and bounds. Thank you, Heavenly Father, Amen."

To be fruitful and flourish supernaturally, you must do your part, which can be quickly summarized into four simple steps:

- You must first believe
- You must abide in Christ
- You must take an action of faith
- You must draw from the resources of God's glory to do the impossible.

Conclusion

This book is, and has been, an invitation to encounter God and enjoy the same type of life the Apostle John describes in 1 John 1:1-3.

> *"That which was from the beginning, which we have heard, which we have seen with our eyes, which we have looked at and our hands have touched—this we proclaim concerning the Word of life. The life appeared; we have seen it and testify to it, and we proclaim to you the eternal life, which was with the Father and has appeared to us. We proclaim to you what we have seen and heard, so that you also may have fellowship with us. And our fellowship is with the Father and with his Son, Jesus Christ."*

This same invitation has been extended to you, so that you can also experience and have fellowship with that eternal life, with the Father and with His Son, Jesus Christ.

The purpose of this book will have been fulfilled if, by reading it:

- Your mind has been renewed and set free from the many blatant lies Satan had engraved in your thoughts regarding God's character;
- You have developed faith in God's true benevolent nature;
- You have been influenced to relish in an intimate relationship with the God that passionately loves you;
- You have allowed yourself to be persuaded to seek God daily, with passion to encounter Him and experience His goodness, which you were created to experience every day of your life; and
- You have now allowed the Holy Spirit to start using you as an instrument to touch others with the power of His eternal life.

God is closer to you than you can imagine. He has given you Himself. God is your portion and your inheritance. Do not waste any longer this precious gift He has given you. As you seek Him, you will find absolute security and be grounded and rooted in His unshakeable Word and His unfailing love. You will enjoy the abundance of His eternal life and His glory, and will become a spring of water bubbling over for others to receive that same type of life.

Prayer

To Enter the Kingdom of God

If you still have not said a prayer to enter the Kingdom of God, at this very moment you can confess it out loud, with faith and conviction to receive the Lordship of Jesus Christ over your life:

> *"Heavenly Father: I ask you to forgive me for having governed my own life and for having lived independently from You. From now on, I surrender myself completely to You. I ask you to govern my life. I recognize that I am a sinner and that my sin separates me from You. I repent for all my sins, and I voluntarily confess Jesus as my Lord and Savior. I believe that He died for my sins, I believe with all my heart that You, Heavenly Father, raised Jesus from the dead. Jesus, I ask You to come into my heart and change my life. I renounce to every covenant I have made with the devil and the kingdom of darkness, with myself and with the world, and I make a new covenant with You, Lord Jesus. If I were to die today, upon opening my eyes, I know I will be in Your arms. Amen!"*

If you earnestly said this prayer, if you repented of your sins, and if, with all your heart, you confessed the Lordship of Jesus over your life with the revelation of Who He is and that He is alive, I want you to know that you have been born again. You have received eternal life and have been transposed to the Kingdom of God and of His beloved Son, Jesus Christ.

> *"And giving joyful thanks to the Father, who has qualified you to share in the inheritance of his holy people in the kingdom of light.13 For he has rescued us from the dominion of darkness and brought us into the kingdom of the Son he loves." – Colossians 1:12-13*

> *"Most assuredly, I say to you, he who believes in Me has everlasting life." – John 6:47 - NKJV*

Testimonies

The following are powerful and touching testimonies shared by women from different nations of the world, that wanted to testify about how much they have been blessed in different areas of their lives by reading the "Kingdom Women" series of books.

Women's lives have been impacted and transformed with the revelation of God's Word contained in these books, not only in our local ministry but also internationally, including the lives of women who have read the "Kingdom Women - Overcoming Crisis" book, translated to Russian.

Lizbeth Aviles (USA)

"I would like to share my testimony of what God has done in my life through reading the Kingdom Women books. First, I want to thank God for what He has done, and also thank you Teacher Ondina for allowing God to use you in ministering to women. I was struggling with a lot of things in my life, specifically with a relationship that at the time I didn't really know what to do with. I come from a long background of lack of identity and low self-esteem. I had a father at home but never really knew what the love of a father was, therefore, I looked for love in all the wrong places, going from relationship to relationship, always trying to fill the emptiness I had inside, yet nothing satisfied me.

I knew there had to be something that God could do in my life, so I began to seek material that would speak to me to lift me up from the circumstance I was in. I felt tired of repeating the same patterns in my life. When they announced the Kingdom Women books at the Deborah's Conference, I knew I had to get them. I have received so much revelation from these books! I began reading them with an open heart and prayed that as I read them, the chains that held me captive for so long would be broken. I began to understand and receive the love of the Father. I asked him to forgive me for all my sins and I accepted his forgiveness as my Father. I understood who I was in Christ... His daughter!

Reading this book, I understood that His love for me would never end, and, that alone, brought me freedom! God's presence was so strong over me that I just fell on my knees and wept and wept; I could feel layers and layers of stuff coming off me, I knew He was stripping away from me everything that was not of Him. After that day, I began to have the fear of God in my life. I began to feel a movement in my spirit and a deep desire to please Him. I was tired of displeasing God, but I didn't know how to stop what I was doing wrong, I couldn't do it on my own. But after I read your book I started making drastic changes, and there has truly been a radical change in my life! I ended that relationship that was displeasing God, I've cut off people from my life that were not edifying me and I've learned to depend totally on God.

I am a single mother of four kids, but the freedom and the love that I feel from God is incredible. I want to please Him in all that I do. I serve him out of appreciation for setting me free from years and years of struggling with all these things in my life! Now I use this testimony to share it with other women who are in the same condition I was in. I am a living example of the true power of God."

Pastor Anastasia Zotova (Russia)

"Teacher Ondina, your 'Kingdom Women, Overcoming Crisis' book was fundamental for me to be able to have the first women's conference at our church. It was the basis for the conference, which was about "Victory Over Difficulties Through Prayer." At our women's conference, many women reactivated their prayer life and since then, they have testified that they have begun to win in many circumstances! Thank you for teaching us to believe and pray!

Anna Alova (Russia)

"This book has turned everything upside down in my mind, soul and heart. My views on God as well as my heart and attitude have been changed since reading it. Now I look upon all spheres of my life differently. Through it, I got one step closer to God. I have been freed from offenses. In the past, when I was told something unpleasant, I wouldn't make it obvious to others, but there was a great storm inside of me. In my mind, I knew I had the wrong attitude, but I could not do anything about it. During the women's conference, a sister blessed me with the 'Kingdom Women-Overcoming Crisis' book, and I realized that God wanted to speak to me through it. My problem with offenses was very serious, and I kept asking God in my prayers about how to deal with offenses. The

Father told me with love, 'your reaction in those situations is not right and I want to free you from that'. When I read the Kingdom Women book on Overcoming Crisis, I received my freedom. I read the following which touched me deeply: 'God does not want you to be upset because of people's actions or their bad attitudes towards you. If God says this, it means we have the ability and self-control to decide how to react to offenses. You have power to let yourself get upset or not! Use it!' I was crying while reading these lines. I got my answer and my freedom from my heavenly Father! Now I can take offensive words and life's difficulties with peace in my heart and with a smile on my face. More love and more faith in God has been established in my heart. Praise and honor to God! He answered, He has done it!"

Oksana Dorofeeva (Russia)

"When I read the chapter in the 'Kingdom Women Overcoming Crisis' book titled: "How to Exercise Our Faith", it helped me to overcome in faith. This chapter says that I can allow my spiritual ears to hear some things and ignore other things. I always had a problem with this issue as I always reacted on each spoken word said to me. The day after I read about the importance of ignoring Satan's voice which comes to rob our faith, I heard some very bad comments made by someone who is very close to me, and I didn't react as before. I realized that I needed to ignore those words, because the enemy was speaking them to me through that person, and I had a right to ignore them. I was so glad to feel free from the hurt and contamination of those words, that I even began to bless that person."

Larisa Medvedeva (Russia)

"I have a testimony connected to the 'Kingdom Women, Overcoming Crisis' book. It helped me to deal with my fears. I went to the hospital for a surgery and I brought the book with me. I had a lot of fears as I was laying down waiting for the hospital cart to take me to the surgery room. In fact I was terrified. I prayed, 'Holy Spirit, help me get rid of this fear!' I started to repeat Bible verses in my head, but it didn't help much. I took the Kingdom Women book and opened towards the back and I read a prayer that released me from fear! It was the prayer of salvation. I read that page, prayed and I fell asleep with total peace. When the nurses came to take me to surgery all the fear was gone."

Jackie Dye (USA)

"Hello Teacher Ondina. I would like to thank you for the Kingdom Women books. Reading these books encouraged me to seek God in a greater way and spend more time in His presence. Your books also taught me how to forgive, how to live a godly life, how to be a warrior in the spirit and how to pray for my family. I've also learned who I am in Christ, because when I was a member of a Baptist Church I was not taught that I had a God given identity in Christ Jesus. I am grateful for you, because this is the first time in six years, since I've been saved, that I am truly sold out for Jesus. You have inspired me to go after souls for God's Kingdom. What God has done is supernatural!"

Candy Arce (USA)

"The 'Kingdom Women, Overcoming Crisis' book has really touched my life and helped me. I keep it next to my bed and I read the powerful prayer in the back all the time. I have even read that prayer over my 24-year-old son when he was going through a crisis. After reading the book, I got stronger in my faith to fight the battles I've been through. I went through a crisis in my marriage (my husband walked away from the faith after serving in church for 7 years). I was left alone in my walk with the Lord. I wanted to just give up and almost did at one time! The Kingdom Women book has helped me see things differently, and pray differently, it taught me to pray with authority and power. Before reading this book I only knew about power and authority, but reading it gave me the revelation on how to use them to deal with these things. Before reading this book, I felt that God could not use me. In my mind, I really thought that, since I'm one with my husband, and he walked away from the faith, that was it for me, that God couldn't use me. However, your book taught me differently. God can use me even if my husband is not following the Lord! God can use women even if their husbands are not doing right. Now, I just pray and turn things over to God for Him to deal with my husband. Also, even though my husband is not at church, I have seen God's faithfulness during this season because God has saved my younger son, and his wife. They were both baptized and now attend church. Thank you for the book. It has helped me to continue to fight the good fight of faith!"

Nydia Rojas (USA)

"Your Kingdom Women books have been a great blessing for my life. Each book has in them tools and practical truths that when I have applied them, they have taken me to another level in my spiritual life. Each chapter has illuminated my way of thinking, which I needed while I was going through a very difficult situation in my marriage in which I found myself hopeless and defeated. Today, I can see these situations with another perspective and although I have not received the breakthrough, I have another way of acting and seeing the problem. I am being changed by the power of the Holy Spirit.

I had never seen myself as a Kingdom of God woman, until now. Now that I do, I also see myself as a beloved daughter of God. These books arrived just in time in my life. Change is not easy, facing our character flaws, such as pride and independence. This change is something only the Holy Spirit can do, and your books helped me to see these things. "Guard your heart because from it flows the issues of life", is now an almost daily request of my heart to God. When I began to read the first chapters of the book 'Kingdom Women-Prevailing Against All Obstacle', it was as if God himself sat with me to explain how to guard my heart from a world full of evil and lies. The book helped me understand what the Holy Spirit was leading me to pray and intercede for my marriage, my family, my calling and my disciples. Now I persevere with a palpating faith, that what I long for I will receive it. Even during difficult times of challenges, I continuously see daily victories. Each book is a treasure that I keep and re-read often. God bless you! I can't wait for the next book."

Jacqueline Hafer (USA)

"Teacher Ondina: I received the 'Kingdom Women-Prevailing Against All Obstacles' book as a gift from my daughter. As I began reading it, my world was impacted by two major points addressed within the book. The first point that impacted me was the explanation of how many invisible barriers can be in our hearts that hinder us and we may not be aware of them. I was able to understand this from your comparison to the sound barrier that was an obstacle for planes to trespass in flight. Secondly, the blindfold was removed from my eyes as to the condition of my heart, when I read the part where you state that "bad moods are the cousins of emotions", because I was always in a bad mood, that had become a way of life for me.

Before reading your book, my life had reached a turbulent state where my relationship with my children had completely been destroyed and lost. Negative thoughts began to penetrate my mind and I began to fall into a state of depression. It never mattered how hard I pushed myself to get back up, there was always a feeling of oppression and weight on my shoulders. I noticed that it became a way of life for me to feel this way. It was normal for me to be in a bad mood. I also began to feel manipulated by certain family members who influenced other family members to not give me love or affection and I became isolated. At this point, I had already lost all authority and faith in myself. I wasn't firm, I became inconsistent, and began to fail in all areas of my life. Although I would pray, fast and do spiritual warfare, these hard situations were not being removed from my life. It was until I read your book, that I received revelation and understood that I needed to do to be free. This book has equipped me with powerful prayers that have helped me remove all these barriers.

I began to realize that you must let God do things supernaturally. The Holy Spirit gave me eyes to see and ears to hear. I learned that I cannot do it in my own strength, that I need to let Him do it. I prayed various times a prayer that was in the book and it helped me remove all the barriers that were in my life. God Bless You!"

Bibliography

Amplified Bible (AMP) Copyright © 2015 by The Lockman Foundation, La Habra, CA 90631. All rights reserved.

Amplified Bible, Classic Edition (AMPC) Copyright © 1954, 1958, 1962, 1964, 1965, 1987 by The Lockman Foundation

Bevere, John. *Breaking Intimidation.* Lake Mary, FL: Charisma House, 1995. Print.

Cho, D.Y. *The Fourth Dimension – Volume Two.* S. Plainfield, NJ: Bridge Pub., 1983. Print.

English Oxford Living Dictionaries. N.p., n.d. Web. Retrieved from: https://en.oxforddictionaries.com/definition/flourish

English Standard Version (ESV) The Holy Bible, English Standard Version. ESV® Permanent Text Edition® (2016). Copyright © 2001 by Crossway Bibles, a publishing ministry of Good News Publishers.

Maldonado, Guillermo. *Daily Encounters with God.* United States, 2016. Print

Maldonado, Guillermo. *How to Walk in the Supernatural Power of God*. New Kensington, PA: Whitaker House, 2013. Print.

Maldonado, Guillermo. *Supernatural Transformation: Change Your Heart into God's Heart*. New Kensington, PA: Whitaker House, 2014. Print.

Maldonado, Guillermo. *The Kingdom of God and its Righteousness*. 2008. Print.

Nelson, Thomas. *The Holy Bible: New King James Version* (NKJV). Nashville, TN: Thomas Nelson. 2005.

New American Standard Bible (NASB) Copyright © 1960, 1962, 1963, 1968, 1971, 1972, 1973, 1975, 1977, 1995 by The Lockman Foundation

New International Version (NIV) *Holy Bible*, New International Version®, NIV® Copyright ©1973, 1978, 1984, 2011 by Biblica, Inc.® Used by permission. All rights reserved worldwide.

New King James Version (NKJV) Scripture taken from the New King James Version®. Copyright © 1982 by Thomas Nelson. Used by permission. All rights reserved

New Living Translation (NLT) *Holy Bible*, New Living Translation, copyright © 1996, 2004, 2015 by Tyndale House Foundation. Used by permission of Tyndale House Publishers Inc., Carol Stream, Illinois 60188. All rights reserved.

Passion. (n.d.) In Merriam-Webster's collegiate dictionary. Retrieved from http://www.merriam-webster.com/dictionary/onomatopoeia.

Strong, James. The New Strong's Expanded Exhaustive Concordance of the Bible. Nashville, Tennessee: Thomas Nelson. 2001.

The Amplified Bible. Grand Rapids, Michigan: Zondervan. 1987.

The Hebrew-Greek Key Study Bible: King James Version. Chattanooga, TN. Spiros Zodhiates and AMG International, Inc. d/b/a AMG Publishers.

To see the complete KJM Publications catalogue in Spanish and English,
find the closest available bookstore, or purchase directly from the publishing house,
please contact King Jesus International Ministry:

sales@kingjesusministry.org – www.kingjesusministry.org